From Fly Creek

Celebrating Life
in Leatherstocking Country

Jim Atwell

North Country Books
Utica, New York

North Country Books
311 Turner Street
Utica, New York 13501-1727

First printing 2005

ISBN 0-925168-99-8

Library of Congress Cataloging-in-Publication Data

Atwell, Jim.
  From Fly Creek : celebrating life in Leatherstocking country / Jim Atwell;
illustrations, Anne Geddes-Atwell.
      p. cm.
  ISBN 0-925168-99-8 (alk. paper)
  1. Atwell, Jim. 2. Widowers—New York (State)—Biography. 3. Fly Creek
(N.Y.)—Biography. I. Title.
  CT275.A879A3 2004
  974.7'74—dc22

                        2004016476

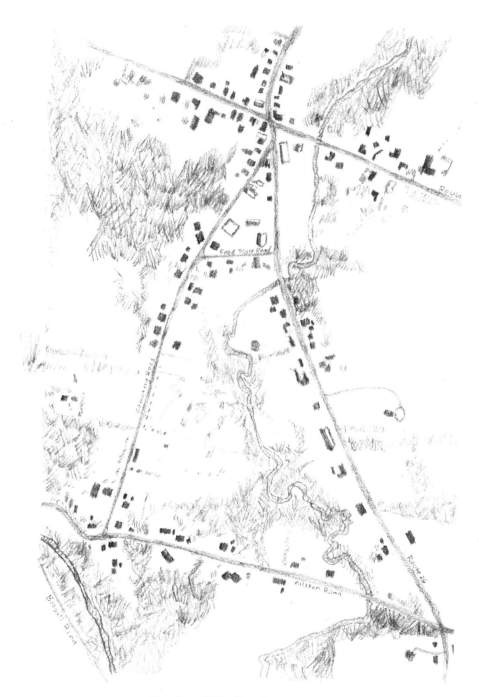

Hamlet of Fly Creek, New York

Dedication

For Gwen who brought
And for Anne who brings
Such happiness to my life.

Table of Contents

Foreword   ix

Acknowledgments   xi

Introduction   xiii

1   History Lives in an Old House   1

2   "Feed a Cold"—and the Livestock   6

3   Farming Like the Big Guys   10

4   Counting Owen the Cat's Lives   14

5   Check the Chicken Catalog   19

6   Meeting Amelia   25

7   About Arrie Hecox   29

8   Shin Splints Aside, a Great Day!   34

9   Skunk Troubles   37

10   Ghosts and Cabin Fever   41

11   Expanding into Pork   46

12   Barnyard Harmony   51

13   Hurray for Early December!   55

14   "I Know Pigs—and Babe's No Pig"   59

15   Ball One!   63

16   Hear All Them Bells...   68

17   Oh, We Like Sheep!   74

18   Disturbers of the Peace   78

19   Old Stones Settle   85

20   Natty Bumppo Slept Here...   89

21   With Hands on Hearts   92

22   Mary's Little Lambs—and Maude's and Maggie's   95

23	Pigs—the Last Act	98
24	"The Diviltries of the Law"	101
25	Serving Up Food, and Friendship, Too	107
26	Two Sheep Tales	111
27	A Woman of Determination	116
28	The Picking Ritual, Getting Outfoxed	119
29	Despite the Odds, Here I Am	125
30	Head Over Heels Over Maggie	128
31	Old Man and Old Dog	131
32	Still Backing the Brave Lost Cause...	135
33	Shall a Hyphen Come Between Us?	138
34	What was Meant to Be?	141
35	Something Left Unsaid	146
36	All the Way Back to Adam	149
37	A Marriage Well Begun	151
38	To Connecticut and Back	156
39	Thanks, Anna and Sam...	162
40	"The Animals are Coming..."	166
41	A Door Reopened, a Lamp Relit	171
42	Eliphalet's House—and Ours	174
43	Raise the (Mailbox) Flag!	177
44	"Long Ago... Far, Far Away"	181
45	"Where'd You Say You Live?"	184
46	Not an Earthquake—Just a Cultural Shift	189
47	Keeping Watch with the Flock by Night	193
48	Two Great Parades	196
49	Following the Sign	202
	An Afterword	207

Foreword

Everyone has a story. Make no mistake, though, finding the story in ordinary lives is a talent. Jim Atwell has that talent. In this book you will find a columnist's celebration of the extraordinary in the ordinary events of our lives. Jim is as comfortable in the barnyard as he is in the university, where he spent a distinguished academic career as a teacher, counselor and dean. It surprises many people that Jim hasn't been a Fly Creek resident most of his life. He so embraces the richness of rural life and relationships that it's hard to imagine him in any other setting.

Jim came to Fly Creek only a decade or so ago. It must have been a challenging time for him. For years, Jim and his wife Gwen had dreamed of retiring to their country home in upstate New York. It would be a return by Gwen to her Otsego County roots; for Jim it would be a new adventure. But cancer changed all that, cutting Gwen's life tragically short and leaving Jim adrift. We all react differently to grief. For some, this loss and disorientation would mark a descent into loneliness and bitterness. But somehow Jim found the strength to begin his new life on the foundation of their old dream—not the same certainly, but in the spirit and with the resolve that Gwen and Jim envisioned their future together.

As you read the book, you will learn how the new beginning unfolded. With gentle humor, endearing self-deprecation and a keen eye for the good and noble in people, Jim celebrates his community. But more: Those who never have set foot in Fly Creek or met Arrie Hecox, will see people they know—or want to know—in this work. And along the way, you will read about finding love later in life. The wonderful, ongoing story of Jim and his bride, Anne, is an inspiration.

Not long after he relocated to Fly Creek, Jim began writing a column for *The Freeman's Journal* weekly newspaper.

As founding editor of the relatively new but successfully competing weekly, the *CoopersTown Crier,* I quickly recognized Jim as the perfect columnist for the Cooperstown area. I was envious. Jim savored the give and take of rural life but was at ease in all parts of the area's diverse, sophisticated community. And so, when the *The Freeman's Journal* ceased for what would turn out to be nearly two years, I sought to hire Jim immediately. I'm glad to say his multi-award-winning column continues in the *Crier* and is available throughout the world on the paper's web site.

The first time we published the column I wanted a tag line to tell readers who Jim is. I thought long about the sentence, and finally selected: "Jim Atwell lives in and takes a cosmic view from Fly Creek." As you read this book, I think you'll agree with the description. Fly Creek comes alive but you'll also get a broader sense of community and neighborliness. Jim Atwell takes a cosmic view; he does it the way he approaches life—with respect and gentleness, with humor and intelligence—and with barnyard mud on his boots.

—*Bill Gates*
Founding Editor, CoopersTown Crier

Acknowledgments

I must thank some humans and some other fine animals. Among the humans, Gwen Vosburgh Atwell and Anne Geddes-Atwell come first. Without Gwen, my late first wife, I would never have known central New York State and, after her death, never moved as a widower to the Fly Creek house we had bought there together. Without Anne, my second wife, I would have lived out my Fly Creek life alone, deprived of all the richness she has brought back to me—and deprived of her illustrating and designing this book. Anne and I both thank several local photographers, especially Selma Shepard, Steve Kelsey, and Franzi Kuhne, whose work appears here and who also inspired illustrations. And Corinne Pollak kindly let Anne draw from Corinne's wonderful photo of her late husband Richard garbed for his work as Clarabell the Clown.

I am also grateful to the editors of *The Freeman's Journal* and the *CoopersTown Crier,* where many of these articles were first published. And grateful to all the Fly Creekers who made me feel at once at home, especially Arrie Hecox, Peg Famulare, Horace King, and Maxine Potts. And I owe deep thanks to my writing mentor and friend of forty years, Professor Richard Fitzgerald.

I am also very grateful to Fly Creek's Pastor Tom Pullyblank and to former Town of Otsego Supervisor Bill Gates, both of whom made good suggestions for the manuscript. Special thanks to Bill, of course, for his thoughtful Foreword. Thanks, too, to my editor at North Country Books, Sheila Orlin, for raising all the right questions and for helping shape my writing and Anne's graphic design. And Anne and I are both grateful to Mary Wright of Cooperstown for her acute final scanning of the manuscript.

Dorothy Blackman and John Chesebrough of Edmeston, New York, helped greatly by supplying bases for some of this book's illustrations; as did George Wyckoff and Betty Smith, and Peter Daum of the Cooperstown Central School. Shelley Stocking, assistant registrar, the New York State Historical Association, also provided materials for illustrations; and I am thankful to the Association for permission to use sketches derived from their portrait of the aged "Leatherstocking" by Jean Bernard Wittkamp, that hangs in the Fenimore Art Museum. Sketches were also derived from the crime photo of Eva Coo's auto, in the Research Library files; and from two objects in The Farmers' Museum collection. Andy Stupperich, Assistant Curator at The Farmers' Museum, helped greatly with arrangements.

Finally, to acknowledge those animals other than human: I'm grateful to Cholesterella, Truffle, Pancetta, and their successor pigs; they've shown me raw energy and true zest for life. And a thank-you to Maggie, Maude, Mary, and their offspring—sheep that have trained me to patience and made me feel needed again. And my gratitude to scores of unnamed chickens and ducks, and even to three ill-tempered geese; they taught me a lot, too. All these barnyard creatures, great and small, brought me back to life, readied me for new happiness. I'm in their debt forever.

Introduction

I don't know why you're reading this page, but I can make some guesses. It's probably safe to say the book's title caught your interest. Maybe that's because, like me, you live in New York's Leatherstocking Country—often the setting for James Fenimore Cooper's popular novels about America in the eighteenth-century.

Or perhaps you just like rural life. Maybe you are already living it elsewhere, or have always wanted to run away to the country (as I did). Or maybe you are just among the millions who've visited Cooperstown and its surroundings, drawn by the beauty, the history, or the National Baseball Hall of Fame and Museum.

Whatever your reasons, I have also made some guesses about you as a reader—and maybe you had better see right now if they fit. While I'm at it, I'll tell you about my subject, and a little bit about me.

About you, I've presumed you *are* interested in simple country life—and also that you're a generally friendly person. So I'm going to talk as if we sat across a kitchen table, both of us with coffee cups in hand.

In fact, most parts of this book were probably first read at kitchen tables, and picked up a lot of cup rings and jam stains. Most chapters were first published as articles in Cooperstown, New York's pair of weekly newspapers, the *CoopersTown Crier* and, in a few cases, *The Freeman's Journal.* When I write in these papers I know I am talking to neighbors and friends. And that's the way I would like to talk with you.

I'm going to talk about Leatherstocking Country, and about life here as seen from Fly Creek, New York. Our tiny hamlet is only three miles away from Cooperstown and the National Baseball Hall of Fame, over some hills and in the next valley. That's just about right. We're close enough to

Cooperstown to enjoy it, but far out enough to be free of the village's faster pace and its pressures—especially during summer tourist time. It gets busy enough over there to require a traffic light.

No traffic lights in Fly Creek. We make do with a blinker out on Route 28, with stop signs, and with civility. And though we don't have a Hall of Fame, we Fly Creekers have lots of reasons for civic pride. For example, this is where the World's Oldest Baseball was discovered. (More about that later.) And right near here was the real Natty Bumppo's last cabin. (More about that, too.)

We're also proud of our interesting variety of people. Among us are dairymen and farmers, craftspeople, retired folk, a few artists, and some engaging cranks. And a good scattering of doctors and other professionals, too. These last go into Cooperstown to work, but hurry back here afterward to their families and animals.

There are more animals in Fly Creek than humans—dogs and cats, of course; but horses also, and cows, goats, geese, guinea fowl, ducks, turkeys, chickens, pigs, and sheep. Not to mention the wild creatures that nose around our barnyards and gardens by night: possums, foxes, skunks, raccoons, deer, and more.

And not only are we outnumbered by the animals, but Fly Creek is also home to far more dead people than living. Those still on their feet number under four hundred, but our half-a-dozen cemeteries have been accumulating tenants since the early 1780s. (My proposal for signs on highway approaches, "Fly Creek: More Dead Than Alive," may yet be considered by the town board.)

The plurality of animals over humans, and of dear departed over the still breathing, both make Fly Creek a pleasant, quiet place in which to live—and from which to view the rest of Leatherstocking Country. My own attitude toward life here is, in a word, celebration. In two more, it's fondness, gratitude. I'm really lucky, really happy to be living in this unique place. And happy that I get to tell you about it.

Finally, something (not much) about me. I'm a runaway. I had two earlier careers, both busy, responsible. I did okay in both of them—oversaw big programs, big budgets, crowds of people. Now I raise chickens, sheep, and pigs. I used to be a "suit." Now I dress in sweatshirts and denims. I don't take myself near as seriously as I used to. That's a considerable relief. Oh, and after living alone here as a widower for a half-dozen years, at fifty-seven I got engaged, then remarried. That feels just fine, too.

Enough introduction. If you want to get a cup of coffee before we go on, do it. I'll wait for you.

—Jim Atwell, Fly Creek

1

History Lives in an Old House

*L*iving alone in a very old house, I pay a lot of attention to its creaks and groans, and think a lot about past inhabitants. My small white clapboard has just turned two hundred. Last night, with central New York at almost thirty below, it complained steadily as hard-frozen ground tightened around the stone foundation. Base sills moaned, as did oak posts and beams throughout the walls.

Complaints multiplied every time the heat came on—rumbles from the furnace in the low cellar, and then sharp protests, metallic and wooden, as heating pipes flexed and the wide wall planks strained, trying to strike compromises between dry heat on one side and lunar cold on the other. The whole old house sounded pained; sometimes I thought I heard a whistling sound like breath drawn in sharply between clenched teeth. It was like the sound I sometimes make after snow shoveling, when rising from a chair.

I lay awake, eyes closed, for a long time under the wool blankets, listening to the house and thinking of those who sheltered under its roof before me—eight human generations, at least. How many, I wondered, had lain where I now did, listening to wind-blown snow stinging the windowpanes like sand? How many births in that room? How many deathbeds, grieved families gathered around the very spot where I now lay? (I opened my eyes warily in the dark room: no circle of sad faces, staring down at me. I closed them again.)

More diverting, how many wedding nights were spent in that room? And, in two hundred years, how many couples, young and old, drew comfort from one another's warmth as the wind blew and the house creaked?

I often wonder about the men and women who walked down my stairs ahead of me; who, in summer, leaned against my kitchen door frame and looked out back, worrying about raccoons in the hen house or ear worms in the corn.

Thanks to some scholarly research by my neighbor Irene Dusenbery and some of my own, I know the names of most that have lived here over the years. I know, for instance, about Eliphalet Williams, who ran a woolen mill just across Oaks Creek. His 1817 obituary says he left "a disconsolate widow bereft of a kind husband... the vicinity of a beneficent neighbor... the poor of a friend in need... the community of a useful and worthy member and an honest man."

I'd like to have known Eliphalet, and his family, too. And the Marvins who, before them, lived under my roof—and under the brand-new United States Constitution. And the Greens, here for thirty years after the Williamses, who read the news

about Gettysburg, perhaps sitting on my front stoop. And later the Spencers, who may have sat there shocked by word of the *Maine,* blown up, sunk.

I hoped to learn more about all of my predecessors two years ago when we razed the old summer kitchen. A cellarless ell off the back of the house, the summer kitchen held one long room and a low storage loft. Its roof was swaybacked, its walls, canted; floors, upstairs and down, gave under foot with an unnerving trampoline-like spring.

"A good kick'll bring it down," said Craig Phillips, the contractor. He wasn't far off, though finally it took some sawing of brace beams and a truck hauling on a thick hawser.

"Watch for stuff under the floor," I urged Craig and his crew. In all those years, I thought, surely a few folk lived here who shunned banks, and may have grown old and forgetful of what they'd stashed under the broad boards. Zinc-topped canning jars, maybe, filled with bright five-dollar gold pieces? And, failing wealth, maybe we'd at least find relics that would help me better imagine the Williamses, Marvins, Spencers, and Greens.

In two days, brothers Craig, Brian, and Jeff Phillips, plus Mike Hart, had stripped the wing down to its post-and-beam frame. In an afternoon they had all the timbers down (I've since re-used them) and were pulling up the wide pine floorboards. And, though there were no jars of gold coins, we were making some modest finds. We turned up a cat's skull, an ivory comb with three teeth left, two rusty knife blades with parts of bone handles, and a heavy pewter spoon.

The spoon, interestingly, hasn't the grace or curve of a modern soupspoon; it can't be balanced delicately across a finger and raised to the lips with hand and wrist alone. You close your fist around this spoon's handle; and when you raise it toward your mouth, your elbow must follow right along.

But more was revealed when the heavy floorboards were pulled away and stacked, enough to stop work and make the crew and me stand, thumbs in belts, gazing down into the rectangular foundation.

The summer kitchen had been built forty or fifty years after the main wing. When it went up, around the time of the Mexican War, it was extended out over part of the yard. And when Craig and crew pulled away the old floorboards and sills, they opened to light three hundred and sixty square feet of Eliphalet Williams' dooryard, framed in the ell's massive dry-stone base.

Inside was a shallow stairwell of tightly laid split stone, built against the main wing's foundation and leading once, likely, to a root cellar. At the far end of the ell, with two of its foundation walls incorporated into it, the substructure of a long-gone building: a heavy base, nine feet by nine, packed with loose stone, that might have supported a smith's shop and its forge. And between the two, chopped down, no doubt, when the ell was built, the tree that had shaded the dooryard, its stump over four feet across. Too big to dig out, the stump had been chopped even with the ell's foundation; one of the floor joists had been laid right across the stump for added stability and strength.

Stairwell, stone base, huge stump. Literary types could find some symbols there, I thought—make them stand for ideas of all sorts. A stone stairwell, its wooden steps leading down to nowhere. A stone foundation, massive, strong, but supporting nothing. An ancient stump, its wood dried and friable as milkweed pods in winter, only its girth to hint at how huge the tree had been, how high.

But I wasn't seeking symbols. I stood looking into the Williamses' backyard, and I thought of them. Men of their time had surely leaned a sweaty shirtback against that tree's trunk, drinking from a dipper and gazing out at half the sunny field still to be plowed. Little boys, of several generations, had crouched grinning in that stairwell, breath held and knees pressed tight in excitement, playing hide-and-seek.

Little girls, trailing wild giggles, had scampered off around that back shed during tag.

There was a woman, I'm sure, who sometimes stepped out to dash a pan of dishwater against the shade tree's bark, who hauled her split-oak basket of potatoes up from the dark root cellar, who called "Supper!" from the back door. And hearing her, there was a man, working in the square room above that back stone foundation, who laid down tools, straightened, and rubbed the small of his back.

A new clapboard ell, the same as the old in size and shape, has closed off light again from that rectangle of Eliphalet's yard. But I still lie in the wintry dark, hearing the house grumble about old age and change, and think of what had been under the floorboards, what had formed a tableau, all those years, in the blackness. I think mostly of that stump, how it bore the squared hemlock timber across it; how its roots had transmitted, deep underground, the thump and shuffle of human feet.

Such thoughts bring a fine, strange comfort on winter nights. And a kind of company, too. In a very old house, one needn't feel alone.

2

"Feed a Cold"— and the Livestock

*Y*ou might want to hold this page at arm's length as you read. I have a rotten March cold, and I'd feel worse if you caught it from me.

I feel bad enough as it is. My nose seized up yesterday and hasn't drawn air since. I'm a mouth-breather now, wandering the house slack-jawed. I ache. My poor mind, which usually reaches out to enjoy the world, has pulled in and curled up between my throbbing temples, just behind dull eyes.

I shuffle along behind that dysfunctional nose, which feels as lifeless and dense as a wedge of cheddar. I pass a mirror, see a wild-haired, watery-eyed creature, and quote Shakespeare to myself: "O, piteous spectacle!" It doesn't help.

And I've worsened things with a twelve-hour antihistamine. True, my poor nose has stopped dripping like a tapped maple; but my consciousness, curled in that fetal position back of my eyes, has developed a second nature. Since I took the antihistamine, some part of my attention has stepped back and now contemplates the rest of me with a dreamy, half-drugged detachment.

And it's that separate part that's in charge just now, giving orders to hands, feet, and the rest. I feel numb, spongy, unsure of my coordination; but that separate self still says to act—results be damned. No wonder that package warned against operating heavy machinery.

Getting up this morning almost didn't happen. I'd sooner have folded my hands on my chest, fled far down some low corridor inside my head and shut off the lights. But I could not. I heard a nagging internal voice—some good angel, perhaps, blowing on the faint embers of my conscience. The voice kept fretting me, repeating two words.

"Sheep," it said. "Chickens."

Oh, yes, the animals. I pulled thought into foggy focus. Animals, like small children, must be tended, no matter how one feels. So I heaved myself onto the side of the bed and sat awhile, head in hands, studying two homely bare feet planted on the carpet. They were mine, I surmised.

Woozy from that damned pill, I dressed, went warily down the stairs, and put on farmers' winter armor: boots, barn coat, scarf, wool cap, work gloves. And then, hauling along a heavy four-gallon bucket of warm water, I headed down the back yard to the sheep shed.

The shed is seventy yards to the south of the farmhouse, beyond the barn, down a toboggan-run of a path that I cut between banks of snow. The path's surface of snow was packed and sleek, my boots have poor traction, and about twenty-five pounds of water was pulling me lopsided as I hung onto the bucket's bail.

And, up in the pilot house behind my unfocused eyes, that half-drugged consciousness was still running the show.

"Open the door," it said when I got to the shed. "Step inside." I obeyed.

Three ewes stood in a tight crescent, facing me.

"Hello, sheep," I said and was answered, as always, by a subdued rumble from back near their tonsils. (Maude, the big horned Dorset, is named—not disrespectfully, I hope—for my Grandmother Atwell, who made the same sound when she cleared her throat.) The sheep's rumble was of anticipation: they knew breakfast was at hand. And not just for the ewes. Ranked behind the three sheep were a dozen hens and a big Rhode Island rooster.

Before I moved the sheep into their shed for the winter, I had cut a twelve-inch square out of its common wall with the chicken house. Now when I entered the sheep shed door, the chickens would come bustling in through their small door, ready to compete for the sheep's feed.

And when I go into the chicken house to collect eggs, often a curious sheep will stick her head in from the shed next door. Down there at the coop's floor level and hiding the hole completely, a sheep's large head is an odd sight. It looks like a hunting trophy that's slid down the wall.

The chickens make much use of the communicating door; they're over visiting the sheep more than they are at home. The sheep's feed draws them in, of course, but it's also their comforting warmth.

Maude, Mary, and Maggie wander the small shed like walking radiators, and sometimes I've seen chickens stand right on their backs, toes clenched into the five inches of wool. Chickens hate cold feet.

Snuffling, I uncovered the barrel that holds their molasses-covered grain mix. (It looks and smells as good as most health-food cereals, but I've held off trying it with bananas and milk.)

Maggie, the biggest ewe, came over and called out to me. Hers is a wonderful baritone "baa" that always cheers me— and did so today, in spite of my throbbing head.

I dumped the grain into the trough, and the three sheep put heads together in a tight circle as they munched. Clucking hens darted in and out among them for the table scraps. I poured the water into the heated tub, pulled down hay into the rack, and stood watching the animals' enjoyment. I felt— what? Still sick and shaky, but useful. Needed.

It was a good feeling. It lasted even after, halfway back to the house, my feet shot from under me and I crashed flat on my back on the frozen path. Even after, breathless, wheezing, struggling to stand, I did a brief Charleston and plunged forward, head and shoulders, into deep snow.

Excuse me, but I'll stop talking to you now. A sneeze is coming on, and I don't want to infect a whole readership.

3

Farming Like the Big Guys

'll tell you about me several years ago. I'd taken early retirement. Thirty years of college teaching and administration done. I was a widower, alone, the worst of the grief over. A very different life lay ahead of me and was about to begin.

The moment called for symbolic action, something that would voice the huge changes in my life. But what? A solitary trek on the Appalachian trail, the old me up into the mountains, a different me coming down? Or maybe a month of retreat, somewhere vegetarian, with meditation, and perhaps yoga and a sweat lodge? What would do it? How could I say to myself, "You're not who you were"?

The symbol, I knew, had to be a good one. For we use symbols when words fail; when what we want to say—to others or ourselves—is too emotional, perhaps too subtle, for words. Well, I found it, by inspiration or dumb luck. I found just the symbol to speak to me.

I bought a pickup truck.

Buying it made practical sense. I was moving from Annapolis, Maryland, four hundred miles north to a small farm in central New York. I'd need a truck up there. And buying it eight months before the move, I told myself, meant I could haul a lot of chattel myself, cutting costs. But more than practicality got me to the car lots, talking truck with salesmen. Something deeper.

In part it was "the Tonka urge" which lives quietly in many middle-aged men. As little boys, we played with those sturdy toy trucks in the sandbox and in backyard dirt. We hauled, dumped, graded, all the while growling noises as deep and loud as treble voice boxes could make. We loved handling those little trucks: Full-sized in our imaginations, they made us feel full-sized, too. Bigger boys now, bifocaled and perhaps even balding, we still pine for trucks and the way they seem to enlarge us.

When I drove the red pickup onto my old campus, colleagues came out to the faculty lot to admire it. (I stood with a forearm draped along the open door's top, my foot on the running board.)

"I've always wanted a truck," said one math professor wistfully, and the other men, every one of them, smiled and nodded. Several had to slide behind the wheel, onto the wide bench seat. And when one of them would grip the wheel, I could see just how he'd looked as a boy—the way you sometimes can when a middle-aged man is at bat in a softball game.

But more than the Tonka urge made me buy that truck. I really had found my symbol. My Gwen was gone from me three years. Now retired, I was free of college titles and duties. I was a man alone, cut loose in the world, heading north for a fresh start. And I was doing so in a pickup truck, cardinal red. (The removable cap bolted on the back was charcoal gray—some yin to balance yang.)

I didn't know what my future would be; only that it was up north and I was going to meet it. I was hauling myself into my future, not in a car, but a truck; dressed, not in coat and tie, but in flannel shirt, jeans, and baseball cap. I was gunning my motor, putting things in gear.

"Step back, please," I told my old self. "This rig's pulling out."

❖ ❖ ❖

Making hay. That is what's been going on these last few weeks in Fly Creek and all over the county. Farmers drawing mowers into fields of bearded grass, then tedders to turn the drying hay, then balers to pack and tie it into seventy-pound cubes or quarter-ton rolls that dwarf man and cow. Farmers hauling loaded hay wagons down dusty roads; husbands, wives, and children swinging bales onto the low end of the elevator belt, dragging them off at the top, stacking them high in the shadowed, sweet-smelling mows. Farmers glancing repeatedly to the northwest—who'd work with crossed fingers if they could, so vulnerable is all their work to heavy, extended rain.

And farmers, at the end of the last hard day of haying, standing in the evening, high up in their lofts, among the stacked bales. Aching, tired, grateful. First cutting's done, they say to themselves. Mowed. Turned and cured. Baled. Hauled. Stored. First cutting, safe in the barn.

These weeks of June, I'm in deep admiration of the haymakers' hard work. And embarrassed by it, too. I'm a pretend farmer—retired prof with ten acres in Fly Creek. I write and do some lecturing, and each year I raise a flock of chickens, some pigs, and a couple of lambs for the freezer. I cut hay for feed and bedding, only a couple acres. I steer a brush mower around and around my small fields, laying down neat windrows. When the grass begins to cure, I turn it and rake it by hand. Then I pitch the hay into the back of my pickup and haul it to the barn.

It's farmers' work, no question, but on a toy-like scale. Sometimes, when I'm raking in the front of my field, I'll hear the cough and deep gargle of a laboring tractor; and over the rise on Allison Road a real farmer appears, his tractor dragging an sixteen-foot hay wagon piled with bales stacked eight high. I lean on my rake and wave. The farmer will always wave back and smile—a bit tolerantly, I think. It's the way a cross-country trucker might wave back to a little boy astride his tricycle.

The irony is greater when an approaching tractor carries a driver a quarter my age: Up over the rise in the road comes

a fresh-faced fifteen-year-old flushed with the thrill of driving the tractor, not mindlessly up and down his father's field but, by God, out on the road, driver's license be damned! Assigned to do an adult's work, doing it well. Tickled to death, but dead serious, too.

He spots a figure near the front of a field—not a scarecrow, but an old dude who waves. And he waves back graciously, but keeps his attention where it belongs, on the curving road and that great weight following him. The towering load of bales looms as it passes, blocks the young driver from sight.

"Man's job, that," says the gray-bearded boy in the field. And goes back to his game of raking.

4

Counting Owen the Cat's Lives

That business about cats having nine lives? Owen's made a believer of me. Except he's now probably down to about four.

Owen's a long-legged orange tom who shares the house with me. He's a second-hand cat, pre-empted from his former home by a new baby. In his new life, he's out on his own a lot, hunting through the hayfields or pouncing at mice in the barn. But when he's around, he's really good company.

A dignified, self-contained cat is this Owen. And he's very quiet—I can almost count the meows he has made since he moved in. He prefers to communicate indirectly. When he wants out, for instance, he simply sits by the door, looking meaningfully at the knob. And he'll sit quietly there until he is noticed.

That's my kind of cat, since I'm normally a pretty quiet animal, too. In the house I read and I write, not notably noisy activities. And if I want to overdose on Brahms, I put on earphones. Not much in me to unsettle a well-bred cat. So Owen and I are quite comfortable with one another. We sit on the screened porch and watch birds, we walk back and forth to the barn together. When he's indoors, he's usually reclining in my company, meditating or asleep.

I really like Owen, and admire and respect him, too. I'd never intentionally scare him out of at least one of his lives. Certainly not by falling down the steps on top of him.

That happened though, within weeks of his arrival. I'd got up in the small hours to shuffle dazedly to the bathroom.

Owen, who'd been sleeping, sprawled across two-thirds of the queen-sized bed, hopped down and followed. I turned on the hall light and watched him pad halfway down the steps, then pause to look back at me. He wanted out. So, hand on the rail, I started down after him. And fell down the steps.

It's hard to exaggerate the noise this caused. The old pine staircase is steep and narrow. Most of my contact with it that night was with heels, and elbows, and rump. I thundered down those steps like a ton of coal dumped down a wooden chute.

I did this in the quiet of pre-dawn, a time when there's not much to hear in Fly Creek. Maybe a dog's bark from far down the valley, or a coyote's yipping, up on Christian Hill. You might hear a random car pass—someone driving to or from duty at Cooperstown's Bassett Healthcare. But never a loud noise.

That night there was one. If the State University has a seismograph, I'll bet the needle trembled. Certainly my neighbors up Cemetery Road must have heard it. But maybe they put it down to distant thunder and went back to sleep.

But Owen, poor Owen! The cat was almost at the bottom of the steps when he heard that thunderous roar and spun to confront an avalanche overtaking him. The combination of sound and sight froze his soul. It raised every hair on him straight up. (Well, just consider what was about to squash him: Owen weighs about ten; I'm that, times nineteen.)

He had vanished by the time I skidded to a stop on the floor. But as I sat there, wondering dully if I were damaged, silence didn't return. I could still hear chaotic sound—but from elsewhere in the house. Owen, the calmest of cats, was in a paroxysm of fear. He was caroming off the walls and furniture in every downstairs room. Chairs toppled, magazines scattered. Then, suddenly, he was galloping past me—an orange bolt streaking up the staircase. The cat was so terrified that he was running out of synch: I could hear his shins hitting the risers as he ran.

Upstairs he continued his wild circuit of the rooms, jumping onto and over furniture, seeking some haven of safety. At some point he leaped onto the computer desk, only to lose footing on the layers of loose paper and fall back to the floor. Claw marks on the desk will always record that moment. They look like the ones Sylvester makes on a cliff edge when the anvil, tied to his tail, is dragging him backward for a five-mile drop. Poor Sylvester…

And poor Owen! When his panic was spent, he retreated deep into a closet for what was left of the night. His owner, shaken but unhurt, limped to the bathroom and then fell back into bed.

The next morning Owen was clearly embarrassed by his loss of composure. He didn't sit with me for breakfast and went out earlier than usual.

I've never once mentioned the incident in his presence. I hope you won't either. (Don't worry about this account. He's bright, but he can't read.)

Anyway, that night had to reduce Owen's tally of lives by one. Let me tell you what knocked off at least three more.

◆ ◆ ◆

Cats' curiosity is legendary and, as the adage has it, has done in more than a few of them. It almost got Owen.

As I've said, mine's a very old house; and for most of its two hundred years, there was only one way into the cramped basement: down a set of outside stairs. When, two years ago, Craig Phillips and his crew did a renovation for me, they built a handsome post-and-beam porch outside the dining room, screened against black flies and mosquitoes. I enjoy entertaining friends out there. When we're alone, Owen and I often sit on the porch, I reading, he thinking dark thoughts about scurrying chipmunks and low-flying birds.

The porch was built out over the old cellar stairs; and to go down now, one raises a hatch in the porch floor. It's a big hatch, heavily framed, and probably weighs at least thirty pounds. (I'm already planning to rig a pulley to the beam above it, for the time when I'm unable to reach down, grab the inset ring, and heft up that weighty door.)

A couple of weeks ago, I'd been down in the cellar, finally putting away snow shovels and also hauling up some folding chairs. I'd left the hatch open when I'd gone in to fix supper. Then I forgot about it.

After dark that evening, as distant thunder signaled a storm gathering, I was reading in the living room. When I heard a crash, I leaped up, knowing at once what it was. That heavy hatch, propped up against the house wall, had fallen or been knocked down. But when I ran out on the porch, my blood froze. The thirty-pound hatch was down. Owen, though only his front half, was sticking out from under it.

The cat, who had been outside watching the night fall, had come onto the porch and seen the open hatch. Curiosity, killer of cats, had gotten the best of him, and he'd jumped up onto the edge of the door. As it fell shut with him on it, he'd tried to jump clear. He hadn't made it.

"He's a goner!" I thought, diving at the door and forcing it up. Owen gave a huge gasp, leaped free. And disappeared.

"He's run outside," I thought, glancing at the open screen door. "He's crawled under a bush to die."

The next hour was nightmarish. As lightning flashed and thunder rolled, I circled the property again and again, shining a halogen spotlight under shrubs and trees, calling the cat's name. I was near tears from guilt and grief. When the storm hit and wind-swept rain had soaked me through, I finally gave up, went into the house and climbed the stairs to my bedroom.

Owen was there, lying in an upholstered chair. He was washing himself. Casually.

I sank back on the edge of the bed, wide-eyed, watching him. He washed his back, contorting himself as only cats can. As I sat down, he looked at me, blinked companionably, and went back to washing.

"How?" I thought. "How had he survived that? How, without a sign of damage?" Now he had propped himself up, pointing skyward with one back leg, to wash his stomach. No broken bones in that cat.

The next day he was out climbing trees as usual.

I can only guess that the crash I heard was the hatch bouncing off the house wall as Owen tried to kick free from it. When he landed across the opening's edge, the falling hatch had followed him down; but he must have caught it with legs braced, absorbing the blow so the door just knocked him flat and pinned him.

Thank God, I say; but Owen must have cashed in a few more of his lives. Now I figure he's down to about three.

That night knocked a few years off my life, too.

5

Check the Chicken Catalog

orget the groundhog. If I want reassurance that spring, sooner or later, really will come, I page through my favorite catalog. No, not Burpee's; though when that arrives (around Groundhog Day, come to think of it), it does get me hoping for bare ground and better times. For thirty years now, I've sat down with Burpee's by stove or fireside and daydreamed about placing onion sets and planting potato eyes and sprinkling tiny black seed for loose-leaf lettuce.

But these days, Burpee's has been eclipsed by yet another catalog that is now my top book for promising spring and a fresh start. It is from Murray McMurray's in Webster City, Iowa—from the country's top poultry hatchery.

In drab Februarys, I now prop up my feet by the wood stove and page through McMurray's book, full of full-color photos of beautiful chickens, ducks, turkeys, geese, partridges, pheasants. It's the chickens that hold my interest, and I study pictures and descriptions of forty or so breeds, appraising their appearance and egg production and weights at maturity.

Maybe, I think, I'll buy a dozen Barred Rocks ("beautiful roasting bird"), a dozen Buff Orpingtons ("stately birds of quiet disposition"), and—why not? Get a dozen Araucanas ("rainbow-colored eggs")!

But I always end up ordering the same thing: Heavy Assorted Straight Run. These will turn out to be roughly half hens and half roosters—and probably five or six different breeds, all of them good meat birds and good egg layers.

I phone Iowa and talk to a woman full of country cheerfulness. Then, come mid-March, I get an early-morning call from our Fly Creek postmistress. She's laughing, against a background of chirps and cheeps.

"Jim," she always says, "I don't know if you're up with the birds, but we are down here. Come and get 'em!"

The package I bring home on the pickup's front seat appears designed for a large Sicilian pizza, but with air holes. The wild cheeping from inside continues during the mile drive home—a disorganized, panicked chorus. I try to offer them calm assurances.

"Hang on just a bit longer," I tell them. "We're almost there, almost to your new home."

In fact, they're heading for their first real home. These chicks broke their way out of shells in Iowa, immediately were plopped into the box, and were on a plane, speeding east, the same day.

If baby chicks had some brainpower, that trauma could crush their psyches. But, after some years with poultry, I don't worry. The brightest chickens are just a cut above your average oyster. Just as well, I guess.

The first year I ordered chicks, I was as nervous as a new father. Now I've got pre-arrival preps down cold. Upstairs in the barn, I cut cardboard boxes and tape together a foot-high draft shield, then bend its ends around to enclose a circle about six feet across.

I floor the circle with plastic sheeting, then cover that with wood shavings. Over the center I hang a heat lamp, the bulb about eighteen inches from the shavings. The effect is pleasing. Under the lamp's orange light, my construction site looks like a miniature circus ring.

As last steps, I cover shavings with newspaper and place small water fonts and feed troughs on it. After I sprinkle a bit of baby chick feed on the newspaper, I'm ready.

Opening the flat box reveals a swirling mass of yellow, tan, and gray. I lift out each cheeper, dip its beak in a water font (drinking's a new thing for it), and loose it on the paper. It runs around a bit, but almost at once begins pecking at the chick food—instinct is awesome.

The newspaper's there, by the way, to keep them from eating sawdust instead of food. Chicks can starve that way. (As I said, they're not top-heavy with brains.) Once they start using the feeding troughs, the paper comes out.

From that point, my job is simple. I feed and water, feed and water—and watch out for what the chicken books delicately call "paste-up"—a sealed nether end that, given the endless eating, can turn a chick into a little grenade. The remedy is to grab the affected chick, upend it, and minister to the problem with warm water and a soft cloth. They don't enjoy this indignity. My part's no fun, either.

Threat of paste-up is gone in about a week. Then, after refilling water fonts and troughs, I can sit and watch the chicks perform in the circus ring as they compete for food and practice their pecking order. They tire themselves out at this, but no longer scare me witless as they did the first year—in fact, on that flock's first day with me:

I'd been so excited about those first chicks that I'd brought the portable phone out to the barn and dialed my old office number at the college. Peggy Bowser answered; she'd been my administrative assistant and lifesaver for a dozen years.

"Peggy!" I said, "Listen to this!" And then I held the phone down, close to the scurrying, peeping chicks. Peggy laughed warmly, loving the idea of a dean turned amateur farmer. My, I wish I could have heard her and her friends at the cafeteria table that noon. My new craziness wouldn't surprise any of them, but it surely would delight them.

After the call I sat watching, delighted, as the chicks scampered around on the newspaper, chirping and pecking. Abruptly, one of them stopped. Its head went wobbly, its eyes closed, its legs buckled. It collapsed in a heap. As I gasped and jumped up, two more did the same. Then three more.

"Dear God, what have I done?" I thought. "Somehow I've killed them all!" I stood there, awash in dread and guilt—what to do? Massage their chests? Try mouth-to-beak? Then, after two minutes, a miracle. I saw the first fallen one resurrect and begin to run around again. The rest followed.

It turns out that, when baby chicks get tired, they just fall asleep. Literally.

◆ ◆ ◆

Fourteen months later, when those chicks had long since matured and the hens were all laying, I found myself battling a bird's maternal instinct. It made me feel like an ogre. Worse yet, I lost.

My adversary was a hen, a plump Buff Orpington the color of old gold. She'd been a pleasant, matronly presence in the small flock, causing no trouble and pulling her weight in the egg laying. Then, around May, a switch flipped somewhere in her dim bird brain, and suddenly laying eggs just wasn't enough. She had to accumulate a clutch, settle onto them for three weeks, and hatch them out. In chicken raisers' lingo, she'd "gone broody."

The first time this happened, I cooperated—even extended her four eggs with six from other nests. (Hens don't care whose eggs they're hatching.) For three weeks she single-mindedly sat there, barely leaving the nest for food and other calls of nature.

Only three eggs hatched (maybe the rooster hadn't finished his rounds), but she was satisfied. She led her brood around the chicken yard for several weeks, until they were adolescents. Then she took to the nest again. This time, four chicks. When these matured, she seemed to settle back into the flock and daily egg production.

But then came September, cold weather threatening, too late to bring peeps into the world. And damned if the switch in her didn't flip again. Back she hopped, into her nesting box, and turned tail feathers to the world.

I tried reasoning, but birds don't respond to logic. My chicken books said you cure broodiness by shock: put the hen in a cage and cover it. Four or five days of total darkness should do. In poultry psychology, forget about Freud and Jung; Professor Skinner's got the answer.

I don't know how long that hen could have held out in blackness. I lasted only three days and then had to let her out. As soon as I put her back in the yard, she walked firmly into the hen house and hopped back into the box.

Perhaps exile, I thought. At first light the next morning I ignored her squawks and pecks and pulled her out of the nest, carried her out of the hen house and yard, and loosed her to free-range in the fields.

That whole day she patrolled the hen yard fence, looking for a way back in. She'd walk along, pause to butt her head against the wire, circle behind the hen house, then butt her way up the fence on the yard's other side. Every time I'd look, she'd be at it. Walk, butt; walk, butt. That fence would give before she did.

I put her back in at dusk (there were foxes and coons to consider), but dragged her out of the box the next morning for another day of beating her head against the fence. Halfway through that morning, however, she vanished from the fence. When I searched, I found her back in the hen house, on the nest. Wait a minute! No breaks in the fence; I'd fox-proofed that. How'd she done it?

I plunked her back outside and, feeling foolish, hid behind

bushes to watch. She butted her way around the fence a couple of times, but on the second circuit she stopped behind the hen house. She cocked her head, measuring the distance to the top of a low hay shelter back there. A sudden leap, much wing flapping, and she was on it. From there she hopped to the low end of the hen house roof, toiled up its slant—then jumped, fearless, off the front edge, nine feet down into the hen yard. She picked herself up, ruffled her feathers, and marched into the hen house.

That's where she is now, tail feathers turned to the world. She's won. As I say, instinct is awesome.

6

Meeting Amelia

The list of famous people who never visited Fly Creek runs to some length. Some have shown up, however. I learned of one who did visit here from my friend, eighty-year-old Arrie Hecox.

Arrie's my neighbor, and my mentor, too. Since I moved up from Annapolis, he's had me in a continuous course on rural living, mostly country carpentry and animal care. Arrie teaches for the pleasure of it—and the pleasure of seeing me hammer my thumb or step backward into a fresh cow pie. He does enjoy that.

Last winter we were sitting by his woodstove one evening, the TV on but the sound off. An old photo of a smiling girl appeared on the screen, her lovely face framed in a leather aviator's helmet. Arrie pointed a finger past my rocking chair at the face on the screen.

"There's the first love of my life!" he announced.

"Amelia Earhart?" I asked. "I guess that you fell in love watching the newsreels in Smalley's Theater." (Smalley's was Cooperstown's movie house, sadly now closed.)

"No sir," he said fervently. "It was right here in Fly Creek. I was ten years old." The story that followed stopped me rocking, from beginning to end.

In 1924 Amelia Earhart was using her brand-new flying license to earn a thin living giving flying lessons. That summer found her teaching at the Frankfort, New York, airport, where one of her pupils was a youth named Fred Wiltse. As partial payment for his lessons, Fred brought Amelia home weekends to his parents' home in—you guessed it, Fly Creek. She boarded there for the weekends of August 1924, in what is now Peg Famulare's house, just across from the Cooperstown Bat Factory.

I imagine the Arrie of that time as a very bright but lonely little boy. After his mother died when he was seven, Arrie's baby brother had been shipped off to the grandparents' home. Arrie lived alone with his father on the family farm, now a heavily treed slope up behind the Bat Factory.

During the school terms, Arrie walked to and from the Fly Creek School. In summer, however, when chores were done, the little boy was on his own. That's what led him, in early August 1924, to walk down the hill, across the dirt road, and up to a young woman in khaki shirt, jodhpurs, and boots. She was seated, reading, under an apple tree.

"I said, 'What're you reading?'" Arrie told me. "She smiled up and said, 'A book about airplanes. You want to see?'" Arrie sat down beside her and the beautiful girl turned the pages, showing him diagrams of planes, explaining how they flew, describing the thrill of flying through fair skies and storms.

The young girl, who was a long way from her own Kansas home, put her arm around the little boy's shoulders; they chatted happily and studied the book through the afternoon. And when Arrie finally walked home, he was benumbed with happiness. Amelia Earhart was the first woman to show him affection since his mother's death. He was a little boy in love.

Arrie spent much of each weekend of August sitting under the tree with Amelia. They read her books, they talked, they walked to the Fly Creek stores and back. One day they stood at a shed window and watched as black clouds and lightning rolled down over them from the northwest. Then, at the end of August, she said she had to leave.

"I'm flying to Ohio tomorrow, Arrie, to pick up Wiley Post. Then it's off to California and more teaching."

"I told her that sounded pretty dangerous to me," Arrie

said. "She asked why, and I said, 'Well, if you fly through any electric storms, you sure don't want a wiry post in the plane.'"

"Well, she laughed and hugged me and said, 'Wiley Post's a man, Arrie—and don't you worry. He's married and won't take me away from you!'"

"I never saw her any more except in the newsreels," Arrie said, looking at the stove now. "She married that man Putnam, and he made her change. In the movies with him, she never had on that little tam she wore, with the one curl coming out the left side. Putnam changed that," he said grimly. And was silent.

"When the newspapers said they thought she was dead," he said hoarsely, more to himself than to me, "I was a man of

twenty-three, married…" Another pause, then he cleared his throat with a mighty snort. "I hadn't cried since my maw died."

He leaned forward in his rocking chair, grabbed its arms, and wrenched it around to face the stove. Silence. It was time for me to go home.

7

About Arrie Hecox

*H*aving now told you how Arrie Hecox met Amelia Earhart, I must tell you how I met Arrie. Most older folks around here know him; he was born and has spent most of his years inside a four-mile radius of Fly Creek. For those of you who don't know him, I'd better give some information since Arrie turns up regularly in my writing—he's that much a part of my Fly Creek life.

Arrie was born into a farm family that had come west from Connecticut four generations before, when upstate New York was still the frontier. His two boyhood homes were farms, the first over toward Wileytown, and the second on a hill just east of Fly Creek. (The second, very old house is there still, right where Goose Street meets Route 28.)

In his early twenties, Arrie brought his new bride home to his own farm, up Fly Creek Valley on Bedbug Hill. Their two daughters grew up there, sharing in a dairy farm's hard work. In later years, Arrie and Lillian moved to the much smaller farm where I met them, not a mile from the old clapboard where I now live.

You already know that, once I moved up to Fly Creek as a widower, Arrie became my farming mentor. By then, he was a widower, too; he had lost his beloved Lillian not long after my Gwen's death. With only a very old collie sharing his life, I think he welcomed my company, especially as a novice farmer who needed teaching. And teach me he has.

Arrie's approach has always been to let me blunder into mistakes on my own. He's at one with old John Dewey, who said education is "enabling experience." Arrie will watch me split and ruin a good piece of lumber or snag myself climbing over barbed-wire; then he'll make his terse comment, always the same.

"Well," he growls, "guess that's not the way to do it."

I'm then left to find the right way, or to observe it the next time he nails a board or crosses a fence.

Hay first led me to Arrie. In 1978, Gwen and I bought Stone Mill Acres from Stan Stucin, planning to retire here. Gwen had spent most of her childhood twelve miles over the hills in Edmeston; and when she first introduced me to Otsego County, of course I fell in love with it. From our Annapolis home, we subscribed to *The Freeman's Journal,* and for five years we watched the real estate ads. Finally we spotted the ad for Stan's place—small house, outbuildings, ten acres of meadow and woods.

Our plans for Stone Mill Acres were simple. We were going to rent out the house till retirement time, while we continued to live and work down in Annapolis. But we needed somebody local to keep an eye on the property and tenants. Further, the place had two small hayfields; if they weren't mowed each year, they'd soon be lost to scrub.

I set out first to solve the field problem. Someone said that Howard Cook, up on Feed Store Road, kept horses and might be looking to cut hay close to home. I stopped by to see Howard, but he had all the hay he needed.

"You talk to my cousin Arrie Hecox," he said. "He milks two cows. Arrie's in the yellow house, 'bout a mile down the road towards Toddsville."

I'd noticed that small farm on walks through Fly Creek—old, squat house set on a rise, with a cluttered porch and yard. Behind it was a set of weathered sheds, some with rickety second stories set at uncertain angles. As I'd walked by, I'd heard cows mooing in one of the sheds. Chickens clucked and scratched around the front porch, and once a fine big collie had come out to the road, tail wagging, to get his ears scratched.

Near suppertime on a chilly fall day in 1978, I stepped onto that cluttered porch and knocked. As I stood waiting, I watched the hens, then turned back to the door to see eyes gazing through its glass—gentle, kind eyes. The door was swung open by Lillian, as dear a woman as I've ever known. I explained that her husband's cousin had sent me down to talk about hay, and she smiled and beckoned me in.

Wood stoves were crackling away in both front rooms. It was surely eighty degrees in there, and the heavy heat pressed against my face like a pillow. Lillian led me into the room on the left—a combination dining room, office, dispensary, greenhouse, and gallery. The five-foot dinner table had just enough surface cleared for two plates and flatware. The rest was buried under stacks of old letters and back issues of *Hoard's Dairyman* and *American Agriculturalist,* plus scores of jars and small bottles. Arrie, it turned out, has little faith in doctors, and didn't have any more back then. He oversaw Lillian's health and his own with herbs, raw honey, and black cherry extract.

The greenhouse atmosphere came from Lillian's houseplants, mostly old and very large. Leggy geraniums almost covered the room's three cloudy windows, their brittle stems following strings to nails driven in the window trim. In that heavy heat, the plants literally gave the room the spicy scent of a hothouse.

The gallery aspect was produced by Arrie's simple rule, probably followed since he and Lillian moved into the house: If it comes through the mail and has a colored picture, don't discard it. Display it. Arrie had followed through by tacking calendars, magazine covers, postcards, and valentines over all the walls—and, in one corner, up and onto the ceiling. A few framed pictures were also on the walls, but these looked like islands awash in the overlapping paper.

By my 1978 visit, not a scrap of the dining room walls was visible; they'd all been covered—and more than once. For when Arrie had run out of space, he'd just begun a second layer. In some spots, the tacked-up pictures were three deep.

Lillian had left me staring at the walls and had shuffled out into the kitchen. In a moment that doorway was filled again, framing Arrie, in bib overalls and fleece slippers. He stood, arms out from his sides, hands curled, head and large torso canted forward, much like a wrestler about to grapple.

That stance, plus his dark scowl, made a daunting sight. He was about sixty then and looked strong enough to wrestle grizzly bears.

I told Arrie his cousin Howard had sent me down, that I was looking for someone who'd want the hay in my fields.

"Stucin's hay," he said abruptly, and taught me his first lesson: Everybody in Fly Creek knows everything. Arrie knew who I was, where I'd bought, and probably what I'd paid. And he'd been appraising me the whole time I talked. Now he cut to the chase.

"How much you want?" he said flatly. That stopped me short—he thought I wanted to sell the hay. I quickly said that I was just interested in clearing the fields; he was welcome to the hay. The scowl changed. It didn't exactly soften, but it became less guarded. I guess he was satisfied with what he saw in me. For my part, I already knew I liked this man.

Almost without thinking, I told him about our other need—someone to keep an eye on rental property. His eyes narrowed a bit. He was appraising me and my proposal. Suddenly he fired a question.

"Can I store the hay in Stucin's little barn?" I said yes, and suddenly he raised a big, work-hardened hand, clamped it on mine, shook it. I foolishly tried to match his grip, but it was no contest.

"I'll cut the fields," he declared, as if Lillian, now standing beside him, was the contract witness. "I'll bale the hay, store it in the little barn. I'll watch out for the property." And so he did, for the dozen or so years till I moved up here.

And, for the years I've been here so far, Arrie's been watching out for me, too. I can't really measure his influence—except to say that he shapes my ways even when he's not around. Alone in the barn, if I miss the trough with grain or drive a nail into a knot, I find myself echoing that gruff voice.

"Well," I growl, "guess that's not the way to do it."

8

Shin Splints Aside,
a Great Day!

All right, I was pretty stiff on the morning after Cooperstown's annual Hall of Fame Game, pretty slow crawling out of bed. But I'd had a great time. What brought on the shin splints (gone in two days) was serving as a volunteer usher at the big game. With about forty others, I'd been recruited into the job by Jeff Hale, United Methodist pastor in Cooperstown.

I've never heard Jeff in the pulpit, but, judging by his persuasiveness, I'll bet he's a corker. As a start, Jeff had roped in about a dozen other Methodist pastors in the area. Then he'd followed the scriptural directive—he'd scoured the highways and beaten the bushes.

When he'd finished his salesmanship, Jeff had pulled in folks from far out in the hinterlands—from over in Edmeston, mind you, and even from Albany, ninety minutes away. At 10:30 on Game Day, Jeff had a crowd of men milling around the church basement, packing away Methodist doughnuts and coffee.

About eleven Jeff turned us over to two local sportsmen. Doug Geertgens and Bob Snyder gave us our grandstand or bleacher assignments, and then raised and answered possible problems: What if someone keels over from the heat? Or sneaks beer into the stands? Or tries to climb onto the field? Or is in the wrong seat?

Luckily, the answer to nearly all these questions was, "Alert your section captain." Turns out, they handle all the real problems. We just had to find our sections ("207," I kept repeating

under my breath) and then steer people who looked puzzled to their proper rows and seats.

Official "Usher" caps on heads, we hiked down Main Street to Doubleday Field. Outside it, the Cooperstown senior class members were manning a half-dozen food stands, raising money for a trip. I'd just read in *Sports Illustrated* that baseball fans eat much more than crowds at other sports events, who mostly limit their concession visits to times-out or period breaks or halftimes. Baseball fans, said the magazine, just munch and gulp through the whole game. So, to get in the right spirit, I had a first hot dog on the way in. Plus a soda. Plus chips. (Hey, it was all for the seniors' class trip!)

At noon, when the gates opened, all ushers were in place, I, high up in the third-base stands, steering people left into 207, right into 208. Early arrivals ate lunches and took pictures. I had time to visit with three Labatt's salesmen, down to back the Expos. (They promised to sample Old Slugger beer, the pride of Otsego County, before they headed back north.) But by 12:45, fans were pouring in, and I was too busy to do more than smile repeatedly, wave a hand, and say, "Need any help?"

I said this mostly to moms or dads with fistfuls of tickets and flocks of manic kids, or to older folks who stood shading their eyes, trying to spot section numbers. I did misjudge one of the latter, a short, gimlet-eyed woman elbowing along the concourse. No guessing her age—in British terms, she'd advanced from a place among the Wrinklies to one among the Crumblies. But when I flashed my smile and offered help, she answered in a voice like the long-gone Tallulah's.

"One side, sonny!" she thundered. "I'm old, not stupid."

That "sonny" cheered me well into the third inning.

The next day's shin splints came from hours of roving up and down the concrete steps, trying to watch the game without blocking people's view. And partly, I think, my legs ached from watching those Cooperstown seniors, making four trips up the steps for every one of mine, lugging cases of soda and chests of ice cream. The day was fiercely hot, a brass-bound scorcher, and people were chugging colas in a single breath and knocking back hot dogs and Ben and Jerry's as if cholesterol hadn't yet been invented.

Those seniors made lots of money, but they worked hard for every cent of it. And I was so touched by their zeal that I bought some food or drink from every pair working my section. I think there were about six pairs, maybe seven....

Well, the All-Star game was great. And shin splints (and indigestion) aside, I'm ready to do it again. But maybe not for a while.

Once a year is just about right.

9

Skunk Troubles

ots of skunk trouble out our way lately. A big skunk has been skulking through backyards on the west side of Cemetery Road, and every night pet owners worry about confrontations. There have been several. The Butlers' dog was hit with an industrial-strength blast and had to suffer a lot of uncomfortable scrubbing; it was pretty uncomfortable for the Butlers, too. Then poor Goldie, Barry Rumple's old golden retriever, got shot by the skunk in her own backyard.

Barry, who usually lives alone with Goldie and an equally elderly cat, had a house full of company: granddaughters Rebecca and Jennifer, plus three small great-granddaughters. He let poor Goldie in around ten, after his guests were in bed, and noticed that the old dog was upset over something. But Barry's nose, he says, doesn't work the way it used to. He smelled nothing—hasn't, for years.

Next thing Barry knew, he was shaken awake by a frightened Rebecca. "Granddad, the pilot's gone off in the stove! The house is full of gas!"

Rebecca had already taken some action. She had awakened Jennifer, and the two of them had begun to take apart the stove, looking for the pilot light. Then she'd called her husband in New Jersey. He had told her to get everybody out of the house and call the police. That's when she woke Barry.

A groggy Barry followed the two women into the kitchen and stood looking at his half-dismantled stove. He explained to the upset granddaughters that the stove had electronic igniters: there was no pilot light. Then attention turned in the direction of poor old Goldie, curled miserably in the corner. There was the source of the smell and the panic. Barry said they lost the rest of the night to scrubbing Goldie with quart cans of tomato juice.

Barry's skunk troubles reminded me of my own last spring, when another hefty skunk was craving my ducklings and chicks. The climax arrived late one night when I heard my seven young Pekin ducks. They were quacking wildly in chorus, though in a half-dozen different keys. I ran from the house with a flashlight and the .22, and sure enough, there was a big skunk, ten or eleven pounds, inside the duck pen. He was walking, very slowly, in a semicircle around the Pekins, who were huddled tight in one corner, blatting quacks of despair.

I clutched the flashlight tightly in between my knees and attempted to draw a bead in the faint light. By then the large skunk had turned his full attention—and also his own artillery—toward me. By luck, I shot first. The skunk rolled over, I went back to bed, and the Pekins spent another hour telling one another what a close call that had been.

In the morning the dead skunk was still there, and I faced

a disposal problem. I didn't feel like a pick-and-shovel job; this skunk had caused me enough trouble already. And I couldn't imagine that Russ Smith would've been happy if I'd put it out for trash collection. He'd have told me to take my skunk—and probably my business—elsewhere. But I needed a quick solution; as the day warmed up, that skunk would start to ripen. So, what to do?

I usually carry such questions to my poultry consultant, George Turner, who lives right across Cemetery Road from Barry Rumple and Goldie. George keeps a big flock of geese and mixed-breed chickens. He has strong opinions about farming problems and about most things—as well he should. This is the man who, with help from Douglas MacArthur, won the war in the Pacific. I've heard the stories that prove it.

In George and Clemma's dining room, there's a grand picture of them on their wedding day, just as that war began. Clemma is radiant, lovely in a white dress and matching hat, and George is quite handsome in his Army uniform. They are smiling happily, leaning into the camera and into their future together. Since that picture, George has put on a certain amount of weight. But that only gives the big man a really magisterial air when he takes on serious questions. Like mine about the large, stiff skunk.

"George," I said, "I've got a big dead skunk in my duck pen. You want it?"

"No thanks," he said. "Clemma don't like to cook them— says it's a mean job to clean one."

"Well, how should I get rid of it, then?"

That steel-trap mind took only seconds to solve the problem. "You got any woodchucks in your fields?"

"Sure," I said. "I nearly stepped in a hole, just yesterday."

"Well," said George, serious as a judge handing down a verdict, "you take your hay fork. You carry that dead skunk to that woodchuck hole. You drop him down it, then you cave in the top of that hole." He smiled slyly. "Then it's the woodchuck's problem, not yours."

You see why I take the really tough problems to George. No wonder he won that war for us.

10

Ghosts and Cabin Fever

At my house, I keep waiting for the ghosts to show up. After all, the place has stood for two centuries. In all those years, certainly some people must have died here and left restless spirits driven to reveal themselves. Living alone with only Owen the cat as regular company, I often listen for them when I wake in the night.

A few years ago, I thought I had one—a ghost, that is. It was just after the central heating was installed, and each night was full of new, unfamiliar sounds.

As I lay in bed, the furnace would come on in the cellar's blackness with a long, deep growl. Then came sounds from downstairs in the dining room—well, all right, from the baseboard radiators. As hot water began to circulate through them, quick expansion produced a sharp, metallic "thunk, thunk, CLACK." It echoed through the downstairs rooms.

To one who's hunted with double-barreled shotguns, the sound was chillingly familiar: two twelve-gauge shells dropped into the barrels, then the gun's breech snapped shut. For a few nights back then, I'd lay in bed waiting, breath held, for further sounds: a presumably homicidal ghost's footsteps as he climbed the stairs to blast me through the headboard, into the afterlife.

After the heating system had had its shakedown, the "thunk-thunk" disappeared, leaving only a fainter, occasional "clack." The sound had me going for a while there, though. And it set me up for something that happened this past fall.

I'd gone upstairs late after working on taxes. That's not a good thing to do just before bed, and it took me some time to settle into a troubled sleep. Then, around two, I came slowly awake to hear a slight muffled sound, like conversation barely heard from an adjoining hotel room.

Except this wasn't a conversation but a monologue—the same phrase, it seemed, repeated. Almost like chant. I couldn't be sure, but it sounded like, "Work, please. Work, please!" It was faint, as I say, nasal and indistinct.

I lay very still, not raising my head. Where was that sound coming from?

My bedroom shares a wall with the bathroom—it seemed to be coming from that direction.

Did I have a bathroom ghost? That would mean a relatively recent one, since the house has only had indoor plumbing for fifty years. But what was troubling this spirit? And why that chanted phrase? I lay there, constructing the ghost's story—what had caused its death and awful restlessness:

Chronic intestinal sluggishness. Days of increasing discomfort. In desperation, a fierce overdose of purgative. Then

wrenching cramps. Then more desperation, more impending despair. Panic!

"Work, please!"

Then some awful explosion—an internal one, blowing out the body's engine room. Corpse tumbling lifeless from its seat, onto the bathroom floor. And now, a specter doomed to haunt the bathroom by night, hopelessly chanting that phrase.

I dared to raise my head slightly, looking toward the wall—and saw a shape. It was silhouetted sharply against the bedroom window's dimness. It lay on its back, feet in the air. All four of them.

Owen the cat was sprawled across the foot of the bed. He'd given a luxurious stretch in his sleep and ended up on his back, feet straight up, looking poised, should the room flip, to land neatly on the ceiling. He was breathing deeply. And snoring. With each cycle came,

"Erk, pease. Erk, pease."

No troubled ghost at all. No spirits of any sort. Only a cat with a deviated septum.

◆ ◆ ◆

Let me tell you now about Owen's state during a recent siege of snow and bitter cold. He got a bit stir-crazy. Between long naps, he'd stalk around the house, pausing to look bleakly out the windows. Several times a day I'd find him by the back door, staring at the knob. But when I'd open the door, he'd just stand, ears back, sniffing the arctic air. Then he'd turn tail and stalk back to sit glumly under the coffee table.

You already know a good deal about Owen, the other animal (besides me) that lives in this house. You know how civil he is, how companionable. And, when not snoring, how quiet. The real, full-fledged meows he makes in a year could be counted on the toes of one paw.

In his stir-crazy state, however, he was making sounds.

Not meows, but odd chirps under his breath as he stalked the house, upstairs and down. I think he was grumbling about having to stay in, and about having to use his litter box, which Owen dislikes as much as I do. He finds it undignified. I find it—well, never mind.

Owen also sounded off a bit whenever I tried to exercise him. The equipment was simple but worked well. I'd tied a length of heavy twine to the end of a spare curtain rod and would trail the long cord temptingly along the rag rug in the sunny back room. Owen would crouch, eyes blackening with the fever of the hunt. He'd gather himself, twitching; and then, with a kind of strangled war cry, he'd pounce.

He'd arc through the air, legs spread, as if throwing himself on a hand grenade. Of course I'd yank the string away and lead him through a series of leaps and turns around the room. It was cat aerobics and made him a calmer housemate for some hours.

Cats, I recently heard on TV, have only been domesticated for four thousand years. Egyptians did it, to clear their granaries of rats. They'd tried cobras, the show said, but were dissatisfied. The snakes were taking out more granary workers than rodents. So they switched to cats.

Only four thousand years! Contrast that to dogs, animals I love dearly. Across ten thousand years and more, dogs have been brainwashed into slobbering, tail-wagging servility. No wonder cats seem so much more willful, feral, closer to the wilds. It's that touch of the wild, I guess, that makes some people uneasy around cats, even hostile to them.

And wildness, mind you, lives even in Owen, most urbane of cats. Sometimes, as he sits next to me on the couch, I'll cup a hand to scratch behind his ears, and he'll turn his head to lick my knuckles (a high compliment, the TV show said, for a cat to pay a human). But every so often, as he licks, those calm eyes will suddenly darken as pupils dilate, and he'll grab my wrist with sharp front claws, grab the web of thumb between sharp teeth.

He doesn't gouge or bite, but for a second I can see in his eyes two cats: Owen the genial, and Owen king of the jungle. Then, with what seems an act of will, he'll suddenly loose my hand, jump up, and cross the room. He'll climb into a chair and sit there, watching me, while the adrenaline gradually ebbs. His and mine.

At such moments I know what all cat owners learn: cats still belong to themselves. One of them will share your life and (as Owen does) bring much pleasure to it. But it will be on the cat's terms, with no surrender of independence.

As I write this on the computer, Owen is sitting on his haunches, as he often does, here on the desk. He's on the right-angle ell to the keyboard and screen; and so we are sitting shoulder to shoulder, I typing and he watching with interest as characters appear and march across the screen. If I pause and look toward him, he looks back with a cat's equivalent of a smile—a slow, benign blink with both eyes.

Why I'm tapping on the keyboard is a mystery to him, as are most of my life and ways. But so is most of Owen's life to me. It's an odd equality that this begets, but it makes us fast friends.

11

Expanding into Pork

I've just been out back, watching the pigs grow. They're doing it with awesome speed—about a pound and a half a day. I only manage that rate once a year, at Christmas. These two pigs do it daily, week after week. Some mornings I go out and wonder if someone has exchanged two bigger pigs for the ones I'd bedded down the night before—some sort of pork-and-switch scam.

I hadn't planned on launching into pigs this year. What with my other duties, the chickens and the half dozen sheep seemed enough barnyard mouths to feed. But a couple of months ago I had a British couple, friends of friends, here overnight. At the breakfast table, young David paused in mid-marmalading, staring out the open back door.

"I didn't know you kept pigs," he said.

"I don't."

"Well, with all respect, there is a pig beside your barn, rooting in the hollyhocks."

And there was. We three went out and found a barely weaned piglet, about fifteen pounds, rooting happily in the soft earth. With a neighbor's help, we got the piglet shut up in a shed. The Brits were enchanted, and I was puzzled. No one for miles kept pigs, as far as I knew. This one must have dropped from the skies.

"Perhaps you're meant to have pigs," said David's Susan, who has a slightly New Age bent. "You must name it at once." Since the couple came from Croydon in Surrey, I told them the pig would be called Croydon, in honor of their visit.

I don't believe pigs drop from the skies as signs, but I was taken by this one. And it was a sad thing to find out the next day (after the Brits' departure) that Croydon was an escapee. He belonged at the Cooks' place on Feed Store Road—had gone over the wall from there almost as soon as they'd got him. Croydon, whose real name turned out to be Binkie, was hauled off home, and I was left pigless and feeling strangely bereft.

That was remedied within the week by a pleasant visit to Hog's Hollow Farm in Burlington Flats. I came back with, not one, but two feeder pigs: one for me and a second for some friends. They named their pig Barbie, but not after the famous doll. Their Barbie's last name is Que.

My pig's called Cholesterella.

Since I'm living alone, of course one pig would have been plenty. But Arrie Hecox says there must be at least two—so that they'll compete voraciously for food and grow all the bigger. Hence the pig partnership. My partners are paying for half the feed, and they also supplement the pigs' diet by cadging surplus produce from friends' gardens. Further, in exchange for an occasional dozen jumbo brown eggs and for some eventual short ribs, Cathy and Jim at the Fly Creek General Store are providing stale bread for the chickens, and overripe fruit and wilted greens, which go into the pigs. How's that for recycling?

Barbie and Cholesterella are penned behind my barn, in a pig yard surrounded by two strands of electric fence. They have a comfortable shed, a wading pool in which to wallow, a four-foot trough filled regularly, large bushes for shade, and an apple tree that drops fruit at their very trotters. It's a pig's paradise out there, and I waste lots of time watching them enjoy it.

The two pigs have the place rent free until mid-November. Then they'll be moving to somewhat closer quarters in the freezer. Conversion from pigs to pork will occur in my own backyard, and some experienced Fly Creek neighbors have volunteered to advise and assist. Dr. Bob Mackie, a respected surgeon retired from Bassett Hospital, has taken a pro's interest in the project. He'll be our attending physician.

Skeptics ask how I, fairly new to farm life, will be able to snuff two pigs I've known for months. I have two answers. First, for a long time I was a college dean. That job promotes firmness and detachment—what job counselors would call "transferable skills."

Second, I've been processing chickens for the last two years. The trick with them, I found, was not to give them names—at least not until it was time to do one in. Then I assigned a name from a list of former bosses and a half-dozen national politicians. That way, wielding the hatchet became fairly easy, and therapeutic, too. (To rid my system of one fellow dean, though, took four chickens.)

Now, after dozens of hens and cockerels have passed into the freezer or across my dining room table, I don't tack on the eleventh-hour names. And I'm way past the sentimentality of those who know farm animals—and wild ones—only from Disney films.

I respect my chickens and treat them well; but know them for what they are: dim, greedy bundles of raw instinct. If I were small or they a good deal larger, they'd gobble me down in a snap. Chickens are interesting, even fun, but no more endearing than Jurassic Park's fierce raptors—to which, it's claimed, they're distantly related.

And I don't expect to feel queasy when processing time comes for Barbie and Cholesterella. They're living, as noted, a pig's perfect life—limitless food, a comfortable shed, soft soil, and mud. They eat, they sleep, they root. And when their idyll ends abruptly, they'll never have known anxiety, want, or fear. Not bad, I think. More than we humans can promise ourselves.

On my part, I'm memorizing the charts I got from the Cornell Cooperative Extension agent, and I'm studying the quaintly titled, *Butchering at Home.* So, when the time comes, I'll be ready.

And the pigs will, too. At a pound and a half a day, they'll break two hundred by late November.

12

Barnyard Harmony

Of course, you know about symbiosis. Back in your high school biology text, remember? Living species, interacting for their mutual benefit. And I bet you remember the textbook examples:

There is the rhino bird, jouncing along on its lumbering host, feasting on nasty parasites it picks out of the rhino's ears and skin folds. And the crocodile bird, hopping bravely inside the monster's yawning mouth, extracting bits of meat from between sawtooth teeth. At once feeding itself and saving the croc from bad gums and costly periodontics.

I thought of symbiosis recently, walking home from Arrie Hecox's farm. He had a classic example going on there for a great many years.

Like most farmers, Arrie's a good slap-dash carpenter, and his barnyard has a cluster of buildings that would stun Buckminster Fuller. Most of the old sheds carry second, full-sized shacks on top of them, penthouses Arrie added to house hay. He's no slave to right angles or plumb lines, and the board-and-batten penthouses yaw and lean in interesting ways. But they're solidly built. The youngest of them has already withstood twenty years of fierce summer storms and drifting winter snow.

The most interesting shed is only about ten feet by fifteen, and about eight feet high. Crouched on its slanted roof, however, is another shed, only slightly smaller and looming up an additional twelve feet. This upper shed is cocked on the lower one at a slightly jaunty angle, like Fred Astaire's top hat. It's packed with baled hay loaded in through a mow door, ready to be dropped down, as needed, through a trapdoor into the older, lower shed.

Until four years ago, when Arrie had to give up milking twice a day, the lower shed was winter quarters for a Holstein and a Jersey. They stood quietly in their stanchions through the icy months, munching hay, their meditations interrupted only by Arrie's early morning and late afternoon visits with his buckets.

Standing outside the now-cowless shed with Arrie, I noticed another architectural detail: a narrow, chute-like construct of boards that climbed the outside wall at a fairly steep angle. It ended high up, next to the hay mow door. The chute was only about ten inches to a side and looked oddly like a miniature walkway walled and roofed against bad weather.

"Arrie," I asked, pointing, "what the hell is that?" His answer carried some slight scorn for my obvious ignorance, but mostly pride in a problem considered and solved years before.

"That," said Arrie, "is my cat ramp."

In winter, he explained, his milk cows needed more nourishment than hay; they also got Coarse #14, a commercial mix of corn, oats, wheat, and rye, all coated with molasses. (My sheep eat it, too; it looks and smells at least as good as most health cereals.) But Coarse #14 draws mice, which soil a milking site with droppings.

If they had their way, crowds of mice would have wintered in the hayloft, enjoying the warmth that rose from twin radiators, the Jersey and the Holstein. The cows' body heat was trapped up above in the big hay bales, among which the mice would have set up single-family homes, duplexes, whole condo complexes. When hunger pangs struck the mice (about every ten minutes, I take it), they'd have staged a raid downstairs and then hauled back upstairs the sweetened grain, all the while dropping dung pellets. Mice scoff at manners and hygiene.

"You need cats in a cow barn," continued Arrie. He didn't mean sleek house cats, but the gaunt, wild-eyed types that haunt most farms, living off the land in the warm months and spending the cold ones, like the mice, hunting scarce food and warmth.

"When it gets near zero, cats need the kind of warmth that's trapped up there," said Arrie, gesturing toward the upper shed. "And the food cats want is there, too—the mice." He grinned. "But they needed help getting up. So I helped them." Arrie had given the cats a weatherproof ramp, built to size. Cold, hungry cats entered at the bottom and walked upstairs to warm fur and full stomachs.

Now, that was symbiosis, I thought, hiking home that day. The cows and the stacked hay bales had kept cats and mice from freezing. Some of the cows' grain had fed the mice. In turn, the mice had fed the cats, who had thinned them out and so protected the milk from unhealthy additives. And, on his part, Arrie the farmer had provided hay and grain for the cows and carried off the rich milk. A grand, balanced system at work.

"Did the cats catch enough mice to live on?" I'd asked Arrie.

"Well, they also got a pint of milk among them twice a day," he'd said. For the cats that had climbed up their ramp also came down again, early morning and late afternoon, to follow their benefactor through the shed's door. Done with his chores, Arrie would splash some warm milk into a tin pan for the cats—and splash a bit on them sometimes, too. He figured he deserved a little fun for his work.

I thought I might tell Arrie about symbiosis but decided he'd sneer at such a four-bit term. And why not? He didn't need a word. He had the concept down pat.

13

Hurray for Early December!

'm looking ahead some months. Sometime in the first two weeks of December, I'll have an important anniversary. I didn't note the date it happened—didn't know, you see, how significant it would be. So, I guess I'll celebrate across the whole two weeks. That way I'm bound to hit the day itself.

I'm celebrating a blustery winter afternoon in Annapolis, Maryland, full of sleet and blowing snow. The old town's harbor is the same color as the sky above it, a grim pewter gray. People on the streets are leaning into the wind, stepping carefully, wary of patches of ice.

Two years a widower, I'm hunched on the lee side of a little red shack near the water, at the foot of Annapolis' Main Street. Next to me is a red Salvation Army kettle; and in my hand, a small bell. Oh, and I'm not alone.

With other service clubs, the Annapolis Rotary provided volunteers to staff kettle locations all over the town. I always asked for the Main Street assignment. The town is ancient by American standards (almost three hundred and fifty, now); and it grew up around its harbor and market area, with streets radiating off to climb hills toward various churches and the handsome, wooden-domed state capitol.

I liked the spot at the foot of Main Street because I could look up the rise of its hill, sizing up shoppers as potential donors. My favorites were parents with several small children. Kids, eyes on the red kettle, would walk crab-like as they dug into side pockets or plastic purses for coins. They'd shyly drop the money into the pot, then quickly retreat behind their parents' legs.

On one blustery day, I'd watched a heavy-set man, red-faced and obviously drunk, weave his way down the sidewalk, fumbling for his wallet as he came. He tacked back and forth from building front to light post, pausing at each to steady himself. The last tack brought him up against the little shack with a thump.

Wallet finally freed from his back pocket, he raised it toward his eyes, riffled through—and pulled out a hundred dollar bill. With a lopsided grin, he held the bill out in the general direction of the kettle and me.

"My friend," I said, steadying his arm, "this is a hundred dollars. Didn't you mean to pull out a ten?"

He pulled himself up to his full height, bridled as if I'd struck him.

"Good God, man, where's your spirit?" he bellowed. "It's Christmas!" And then he thrust the crumpled bill at the pot, almost knocking over its tripod.

Chastened, I steered his hand to the slot; and in went the bill. He smiled at me in woozy triumph.

"So there!" he shouted. "And a Merry Christmas!"

I wished him the same, and then I watched uneasily as he reeled off toward the harbor. Thank goodness, he managed to change course before he got near the bulkhead and that freezing water.

Well, anyway, that's why I always vied for that downtown assignment. But it turned out someone else liked it, too. And in December 1992, the pair of us were assigned to ring our bells together through the cold afternoon.

I'd known this woman by sight from Rotary; but it's a big club in Annapolis, and we'd hardly done more than say hello. Now, both extended time and shared discomfort were ours. And the first thing I noticed was how good-humored she was about the weather. (It turned out she'd grown up in Calgary—out where they manufacture the "Alberta Clippers.")

We shivered, laughed, talked, and enjoyed the little kids and the midshipmen (just bigger kids, really, themselves). We even handled a couple of happy drunks, though none to match the hundred-dollar one.

By the end of our shift, though, we were benumbed. It was four-thirty, almost dusk; snow was falling steadily. When I suggested Irish coffee, she didn't just say yes. She gave a cheer. I liked this girl!

We walked to a Main Street bar, huddled over steaming cups, talked some more. I drove her home in the pick-up truck I'd already bought for the move to Fly Creek. And we began to date.

So I owe my knowing Anne to Annapolis Rotary, and to the Salvation Army, and, I guess, to the cold and snow that day. And that gives me a lot to celebrate in early December.

14

"I Know Pigs—
and Babe's No Pig"

*Y*ou are probably tired of hearing about my pigs. I've already spent a lot of space describing the pair living behind my barn and my plans to convert them into pork, come late November.

Since my first pig column appeared, I've been stopped a dozen times by folks who've asked after the animals. Some have been acquaintances, but others were strangers. That's what happens when your picture's published with a column—anonymity's gone for good. Last week, outside the Milford post office, a guy in a rusty pick-up slowed down to yell, "How's them pigs?" It's got me uneasy—almost afraid to page through a *Playboy* in a store, for fear I'll be recognized and reproached.

Just after the first article, I was in the Cooperstown Great American supermarket, ambling along with my plastic basket. Right in the dairy aisle I was stopped by a woman of generous build in some sort of sports garb—lots of colorful spandex, some of it under heavy strain. She braked her loaded grocery cart and squinted down its length at me.

"Aren't you the one who wrote about the pigs?"

I couldn't read her tone, but her cart was pointing right at me. (Was that costume racing chic? If I owned up, would she slam the cart into first gear and knock me into the cottage cheese?) Meekness seemed the safest option. So I nodded and smiled—and was relieved to see her smile, too, though reproachfully.

"I liked reading about the pigs—but, honestly, how can you think of killing them?"

"Well," I began—but was stopped by her wagging finger.

"You ought to rent *Babe,*" she said. "That will change your mind about pigs." Then, shaking her head, she pulled around me and was gone, cornering sharply down by milk, yogurt, and orange juice.

Well, I did rent *Babe.* My mind wasn't changed, but if I meet the spandex lady again, I've got an answer now.

As you probably know, *Babe* is an Australian film, a gentle fantasy about a piglet won by an old sheep farmer at a county fair. On his farm, the orphan piglet is adopted by a mother sheep dog and soon has identified with her species rather than his own.

He develops a powerful, and seemingly absurd, aspiration: the piglet wants to herd sheep with the "other" dogs. I should note that all of the farm animals in the movie converse with one another, except for

the sheep, who, though very dumb, are snobs. (That's not an unusual pairing, come to think of it.) The sheep only talk to other sheep—until the friendly piglet takes a hand (trotter?) in the matter.

The pig, whose name, of course, is *Babe,* wins the love of all the animals, snobbish sheep included, simply by the milk of porcine kindness. And at the picture's end—well, I won't tell you. Rent it. You'll love it.

By the way, *Babe* isn't an animated film: all the animals are played by real animals. By technical tricks, their mouths are made to move in synch with dubbed-in speech—like Mr. Ed, but a hundred times better.

I'd like to tell the spandex lady that *Babe* is a fable, latest in a long line that stretches back to Aesop, includes Chaucer and de la Fontaine—and, of course, E.B. White's *Charlotte's Web* and Orwell's *Animal Farm.* As you know, a fable is a story with a moral. Its characters are usually animals, but ones that talk and act like humans. And that's the point—not to present animals' behavior, but to highlight human behavior by projecting it onto animals.

Of course it would be hard to butcher Babe; that pig is a complete catalog of human virtues: love, loyalty, bravery, fortitude, compassion... Like everyone who sees the film, I was taken by the pig, feared for his safety, rejoiced in his triumphs. At the end, I felt like cheering.

But after watching the film, I went out and took a look in the pigpen. There, looking back at me, were Barbie and Ella, who embody, not human, but pigly nature. They grunt, squeal, wallow. They battle fiercely over food. In short, they behave like pigs, not humans; and though they are interesting, even entertaining, they are not cuddly or cute. And they aren't filled with virtue.

A case in point: One morning I went out to feed them and found that a brown sparrow had landed on the upper strand of electric fence. That shouldn't have troubled the little bird, but it must have preened its beak against the fence post and grounded itself. As a result, it was hanging upside down from the wire, quite dead.

I took a stick and knocked the tiny corpse free. It fell into the pen, practically at the feet of Ella, who looked at it closely.

Under similar circumstances, Babe would have wept over the little creature. Perhaps he'd have scraped out a small grave with his trotter, summoned the other animals, reduced them to tears with heartfelt words of tribute and farewell. That's the way Babe would treat the little dead bird.

Ella ate it.

15

Ball One!

*M*y fortune's made. Fate decided it's finally my turn and is about to dump a bundle in my lap. The big problem will be how to spend all the money. But I'll manage it.

As I've already told you, I've retired from work in suburban Maryland and moved to Fly Creek, New York, to live in a 1794 farmhouse bought some years ago with an eye to country living. There are woods and two pastures, a barn and a pig sty, a chicken house and a sheep shed. But it's the farmhouse that will make me rich—specifically, the attic. I'll explain:

Fly Creek is three miles northwest of Cooperstown, three miles from the front door of the National Baseball Hall of Fame and Museum. Baseball faithful flock there by the tens of thousands—and I have a way to lure them over the hills, down into Fly Creek Valley, and up into my attic.

A few years ago, a national magazine published a color spread on Cooperstown, illustrating the beauty of Otsego Lake and the village's architecture, and dilating on one of the main attractions, the Hall of Fame. The text retold the shaky legend of Abner Doubleday laying out the first baseball diamond in a Cooperstown cow pasture and then commented, aptly, I thought, that it didn't much matter whether Abner really did. The national pastime really deserves a quintessential hometown, and Cooperstown is just that.

More important, the article implied, people need myths; not falsehoods, mind you, but stories that hold the truth of what we believe about ourselves and our culture. The story of young Abner Doubleday, future Union general and Civil

War hero, applying a keen mind to create a wonderful game, has two qualities we'd like to think are typically American: inventiveness and love of fun.

So, whatever the historical facts about baseball, we'd prefer to have it that Abner created the game, that the national pastime should have its own founding father. But, back to my future fortune:

In talking about the National Baseball Hall of Fame and Museum, the magazine article described one of its precious relics, a worn orb of darkened horsehide, stitches split apart enough to reveal its core of hard-packed wool. Echoing the relic's Museum placard, the article said this was an old, *olde* local baseball.

Perhaps it was even the original, Ball One, a relic on the order of Betsy Ross' flag. Abner himself may have wrapped fingers around that ball long ago, maybe even discovered through it how spit affects line of flight. But now the important part:

This ancient baseball was found, the article said, in a trunk—in a farmhouse attic—in Fly Creek, New York. The house was otherwise unspecified.

Well. We're already in the realm of myth here, remember. So there's no reason why mine shouldn't have been the farmhouse. It's plenty old enough, and topped by just the sort of attic in which an ancient baseball ought to have been found: lots of cobwebs, hand-sawn roof beams with pegged joints, pine floorboards fourteen inches wide and carpeted with dust.

Cluttering the attic are stacks and heaps of gear that house sellers through two hundred years couldn't face clearing out. And so they each said, smiling slyly to two hundred years of buyers, "You're welcome to the stuff in the attic."

I imagine that's what the widow of the miller, Eliphalet Williams, said when she sold the place before the War with Mexico. I know that's what old Stan Stucin said when he sold it to me in 1978. No telling how much Stan and his family added to the attic in their thirty years of living under it. His daughter's schoolbooks are up there, and a box of 1940's income tax returns, and Stan's First Communion certificate, issued before the Yanks went "Over There."

Other items are harder to date. There's an elaborate bird-cage wrapped in Depression newspapers, and an enormous wooden crate addressed to a local who died, I have been told, during Cleveland's second term. And there's a large, battered old tin trunk...

Now, I'll remind you again that we're dealing with the power of myth here. That old trunk's just the sort from which a precious bit of sports history should have been raised reverently to the light. So why shouldn't the baseball faithful, for a modest offering, climb my crooked stairs to gaze, awestruck, at my dim attic and my tin trunk, open and dramatically spotlighted?

And there'll be more for them. Downstairs, I'll have smashed a pane in a parlor window from the outside, and fans will con-template exactly the kind of damage that could have been done by the First Baseball that might have been found up in the attic. They'll be invited to consider that through that very win-dow sash the very first mother ever enraged by such destruc-tion may well have shrieked,

"You, boy! Come in here this instant! Don't you dare run away!"

Out back I'll have laid out a diamond in the hayfield, marking the bases with dried cow pies as Abner Doubleday surely did (if he did) in Cooperstown. Kids, for a small fee, will be able to step up and take a swing at a replica Ball One (locally sewn), and then scamper around the cow pies to slide home.

Other copies of the First Ball, as well as more dried cow pies (local products, too) will be on sale in a modest gift shop tended by me. I'll be in costume, I think, probably homespun

bib overalls and straw hat, with some wire-rim glasses worn far down my nose. And why not? Perhaps I'll add a canvas apron smudged with flour and be old Eliphalet the miller himself. I'll sit on a keg and tell wide-eyed tykes and smiling moms and dads about how the First Ball was made, and about that First Game so long ago.

There's a lot to work out yet—roadside signs, parking lots, food concessions, restrooms. But it'll be a fine public service and worth all the work. For we the people need our myths as much as history.

And, besides, I'll make a bundle.

16

Hear All Them Bells...

*n*ote to myself: "Phone John Meneely in Annapolis. Found him another one." My friend John will be especially pleased with this one, I know.

I was down at Barry Rumple's house the other day, puzzling with Barry over his brand new answering machine. It's one of the new, simplified ones, with all functions assigned to only two buttons. Once you figure out the patterns, using it is child's play.

Maybe we needed a child.

An answering machine is essential to Barry, who gets lots of calls. At eighty-eight, he's as active as anyone in Fly Creek—steadily involved in distribution of Meals on Wheels and a regular volunteer at Bassett Hospital. While we tinkered with the infernal device, Barry told me more about some other continuing work.

Barry belongs to the Baptist church in Worcester and, as its historian, he's just completing an update of church history for its 150th anniversary. I paged through the book and spotted the following: "Our church bell... bears the inscription 'From Meneely's Foundry, West Troy, N.Y., 1851.'"

Bingo! Another bell for my friend John Meneely to list. Until it closed in 1952, John's ancestors ran that bell foundry in Troy. For a hundred and sixty-seven years, the foundry shipped church bells all over the country, and indeed around the world. (One legendary company employee, an expert bell rigger, personally hung more than two and a half million pounds of bells, just in the United States.)

John has the company's installation records, but he loves confirmation that bells hung across all those years are still pealing melodiously. He'll be very glad to hear about Second Baptist, in Worcester. I had another scoop for him two years ago: Every Sunday morning, one of his family's bells rings out over Fly Creek.

Interestingly, the bell in our Fly Creek United Methodist church doesn't belong to the congregation, but to the hamlet itself. Each of us Fly Creekers, I guess, owns a part interest. Florence Michaels, Fly Creek's own historian, gave me the significant details.

Fly Creek bought its first bell in 1841 and hung it in the steeple of the almost brand-new Methodist church building. That first bell, which cost $173, proved unsatisfactory, and an 1848 community meeting voted the purchase of another bell—from Andrew Meneely in Troy. (I wonder, was the new bell hung in time to be clanged for the end of the Mexican War, that same year?)

Here's a modern note: Mr. Meneely accepted the first Fly Creek bell as a trade-in, and knocked $152.82 off the purchase price of $287.83, plus another $20 for a new, larger yoke. (Florence found no mention of sales tax.) That generous trade-in suggests that the first bell was in no way defective. Probably it just wasn't big enough for its voice to carry to outlying farms, up and down the valley. The second bell, at 1,028 pounds, did the job and is still doing it nicely.

The original ringing schedule called for community peals at sunrise, noon, and nine P.M., six days a week; and churchly peals at ten and ten-thirty on Sunday mornings. That nine P.M. ringing, Florence Michaels told me, at times served as an official curfew, to toll "the knell of parting day."

Well, John will be pleased to learn about the Worcester bell; he certainly was about Fly Creek's. Two years ago he wrote, "Fly Creek sounds like a wonderful place to be—especially with the Meneely bell." Then he added a businessman's note.

"I'm delighted that you approve of its tone and that it still functions regularly.... I'm sure it is out of warranty by now."

Not to worry, John. We aren't giving it up, even on a trade.

◆ ◆ ◆

Well, the more I thought about that 1848 bell hanging high in the Fly Creek church, the more firmly convinced I was: I should climb up inside the steeple. I could get a photo of the old bell for John Meneely and send it to him, down south in Annapolis.

I'd broached steeple-climbing once before to Rev. Horace King, the very good-hearted man who is pastor, not just to his Methodist flock, but to all us Fly Creekers.

"Why don't we climb the steeple sometime, Horace?" I'd asked. It sounded like fun to me.

Horace had answered me with a pleasant, non-committal laugh. (That's a useful reaction for clergymen. I think it's taught in seminary.) Then his wife Marie had volunteered that, if we did it, we'd be challenged by more than steep ladders and vertigo. About fifteen years back, a work party of Methodist men had literally shoveled the steeple's platforms free of bat droppings. By now, said Marie, the bats would have buried them again.

But excited now by my new information about the bell, I telephoned Horace and again proposed we scale the heights together. "When?" he asked, to my delight.

"Now?"

"All right," he said resignedly.

He's a really good sport, this Horace. As we walked from parsonage to church, both dressed in scruffy clothes, he volunteered that he really doesn't like heights.

"That's all right," I said. "I don't either." (Horace and I are, after all, both bookish, middle-aged men, settled in habit. We're not inclined to steeple-jacking or rock climbing.)

"No need," I added, "for you to climb all the way up. You can stay near the bottom—to call the rescue squad if it's needed." We both laughed heartily, but I still had a quick, unnerving image of myself, hurtling headfirst downward in a whirlwind of bat guano.

Inside the church, sexton Andy Gracey was sweeping up, and Horace told him we were on our way up the steeple. With a grin and a glint in his eye, Andy said to yell when we were at the top, so he'd know when to pull on the bell rope.

First we two faced the steep steps up to the church gallery. Then we struggled together to drag down from the gallery's ten-foot ceiling a set of folding stairs. Once at their top, I stood in a dark compartment that reeked of fetid bat poo. Then I pushed my way through a narrow door and started up yet another flight of almost vertical steps.

That good man Horace, his loyalty conquering his dread, climbed up the first flight as I went up the second. Then he crept up the second while, above him, I stepped shakily into a high, square chamber just below the bell level.

In this box-like space, there was no flat floor—the pitch of the church's roof jutted up into the room. One climbed the pitch to reach the bottom of a spindly wall ladder. We eyed that ladder. It had been repaired many times, though maybe not since McKinley was shot.

"Why don't you wait here, Horace, while I climb up?" I said. Horace agreed—a bit quickly, perhaps. I crept up the pitch and stepped onto the rickety ladder. Below, Horace kept himself busy—he knows lots of prayers by heart. But he also watched my steps closely, directing just where I should next put my foot.

At the top of the wall ladder was a trapdoor, and beyond it was the bell. But what else might be up there? What about Marie King's bats? Their rank stench was thick enough to be a taste as well as a smell. Would I put my head through the hatch and into the bats' bedroom? Would they be pleased to see me?

I raised the hatch warily and peeked through the crack, glanced left and right. I saw a long-dead pigeon, but no bats, at least in my line of vision. I decided not to glance up toward the highest, darkest recesses of the steeple top.

I climbed warily through the square hatch—and faced the Meneely bell, mute in the dimness. It was mantled in white pigeon droppings, but majestic. If Andy pulls that rope now, I thought, I'll be deaf as Quasimodo.

Andy didn't, of course, and Horace and I made it safely all the way back down. My only heart-stopper was when a ladder rung pulled free in my right hand. I had stepped on it only seconds before.

In the gallery, we both slumped heavily into chairs, excited, a little weak-kneed—but feeling an added, quite satisfying bond. Perhaps that wasn't Everest we'd climbed, but it was more than enough.

I didn't, however, get my photo for John Meneely. It turned out that the top chamber was too cramped to permit it. But I saw his great-great-grandfather's fine bell, and I patted its cold surface for John.

That'll have to do.

17

Oh, We Like Sheep!

If I had not been misled by a sacred song, I probably wouldn't be keeping sheep now. Maybe I am kin to the little boy whose favorite hymn was the one about that funny bear named Gladly. (You must surely remember—"Gladly, the Cross-Eyed Bear...")

In my case, it wasn't a hymn, but Handel that misled me. Oh, all right, that I misunderstood. Through all my early Christmases, I was thrilled by that barn-burner chorus early in *The Messiah,* "All We, Like Sheep." Except I always heard it as "Oh, We Like Sheep!"

It was mostly Handel's fault. He was working, after all, with a pretty sober text: "All we like sheep have gone astray, every one to his own way..." That ought to call for a minor key, I'd think, and a somber tempo. But Handel set the first four words to "doh-FAH-RE-DOH," a sprightly, chipper progression that could open a Sesame Street song. (And the carefree melody that carries "Every one to his own way" still reminds me of Disney's dancing "Three Little Pigs"—at least the two lazy ones.)

Anyway, through childhood, I'd wait through the Overture and "Comfort Ye," impatient for that mighty chorus. Then, in star-spangled polyphony, seeming hundreds of singers would thunder (I thought), "Oh, we like sheep!" And when the orchestra repeated the melody, I'd echo, "Oh, I like 'em too!"

And now I'm raising them.

And waiting for my first lambs to arrive. I've almost memorized the sheep book's obstetrics chapter. I've assembled and carefully packed my kit of delivery supplies. And now I wait. Impatiently. Nervously.

But not without support. Close at hand is my ready reserve, The Leatherstocking Sheep Association. Collectively, its members have delivered legions of sheep—enough, probably, for all the state's insomniacs to count.

It turns out that, among the many other interesting things tucked into our beautiful Chenango, Delaware, and Otsego hills, are about forty farms raising sheep. Some folds, like mine, have only a few. Other owners, like my neighbors the McCormacks at Waterwheel Woodworks, number their sheep in the hundreds. Many use the Association to sell fleeces to the Southern Tier Wool Pool. Some do their own spinning, and even weave, producing beautiful finished work for shops and craft fairs. They're a varied lot, but all interesting, off-beat, agreeable people—and very generous in offering their help to a nervous novice.

My friend Anne Geddes was recently up from Annapolis. (We've been doing a lot of visiting, she here, I down there.) Anne went with me to a Sheep Association Meeting. She tells her Maryland women friends she can always count on some unusual entertainment on her visits. When, looking ahead, she asked some of them what she should wear up here to a pig slaughtering, one said flatly, "A shower curtain."

We drove to Garrattsville that foggy evening, unsure of what to expect. Well, it was more than worth the drive.

About twenty people had gathered in the New Lisbon Town Hall. Two of them, the Opderbecks, from here in Fly Creek, were also new to sheep raising. The rest were veterans, some with very large flocks. This was a denim-and-flannel shirt crowd, and everyone seemed at ease with themselves and with life. (I'm not sure whether that comes of raising sheep, or whether easy-going folk just tend toward shepherding.) The other thing we shared, I noticed, was a faint scent of lanolin.

The evening's program centered on a videotape on ovine

birth problems, featuring a wizened Indiana vet who looked old enough to have treated sheep for Abraham, Isaac, and Jacob. Lecturing in a barn, in front of piled bales of hay, the old vet proudly displayed a visual aide of his own making. It was a transparent plastic box, oblong, about the size of a sheep's body. Inside he had installed plastic partitions to represent a ewe's birth canal and pelvic structure. It was all straight lines and right angles, but you got the idea.

Using the box, plus a cute toy lamb that was meant for a sleeping baby's crib, the old vet demonstrated how a well-bred sheep enters the world. (Like a diver—head down, front legs forward and together.) But then he contorted the floppy lamb into a half-dozen hapless variations. In each case, he put the toy into the plastic box and showed how it jammed and wedged against the various partitions.

Whoa! I sat there slack-jawed, imagining me facing mis-aligned head and limbs—and rearranging them from the outside in, as it were. Then the old vet switched from plastic box and floppy toy to the real thing: a series of grim film clips of him dealing with lambs in bad trouble and ewes in real distress. In the film he demonstrated an intervention for each problem, and to everyone's relief got all the lambs into the light of day.

Periodically during the old vet's presentation, the videotape was stopped by the man who'd brought it to Garrattsville. He's a young vet obviously much liked by the sheep raisers: David Leahy of Otego. Dr. Leahy would push the pause button to stress a point just made by his elderly colleague—and sometimes to contradict him.

In the latter cases, he often asked someone in the audience how she or he would handle the problem. At first I thought he was asking questions to make people think, but that wasn't it. The doctor was deferring to individuals who'd delivered far more lambs than he had. This impressive, good-humored man was not a bit concerned about vaunting his own professional status; he just wanted everyone to know how to do the job right. Good for Dr. Leahy, I say.

Late in the live-action segment, after the tape had been paused uncomfortably long on a prolapse, I was suddenly sure I didn't want to face lambings alone, year after year. Just then Dr. Leahy said that, if someone has to reach in to help a lamb out, a woman is usually better: her hand's typically smaller. I reached over, raised Anne's hand, and placed her palm against mine. Sure enough. Hand for hand, she's really better suited for the job.

For other, far better reasons than that, I proposed that night, back at the house. Anne said yes. What a team we're going to make!

And Anne's coming back up here from Annapolis for Easter weekend. By luck or providence, that's just about when the ewes are due!

18

Disturbers of the Peace

tricky job, with a couple of factors working against us. But probably we could handle it. With Arrie in charge, success was almost guaranteed.

Dr. Claire Beetlestone had phoned from the Montessori School in Toddsville. The place was under siege by geese. Someone thought a few geese around the school would add a scenic touch and give the kids something fun to watch. But the birds had become a curse.

Big, messy creatures, they weren't satisfied just to glide picturesquely on Oaks Creek. No. The five forged ashore like an expeditionary force and waddled right up to the school, invading the kids' play areas. When they waddled back, they left worse than a few loose feathers.

The staff decided the geese had to go. There are no Goose Busters in Greater Otsego, so I got the call. My own fault, I guess, for writing so much about my ducks, chickens, sheep, and pigs.

Driving down to Toddsville, Arrie Hecox and I discussed the two challenges. The first was just getting hold of the geese. They're wily birds, and hostile by nature, with wings strong enough to break a grown man's wrist. We'd have to be stealthy, guarded.

The second factor was the school's kids. Many of them, I told Arrie, would have seen *Fly Away Home,* a lovely, lyrical film about a little Canadian girl's rescue of wild geese she's hatched out. Amy Alden has to teach them to fly south, or they'll be snatched by the Ontario geese police and sold, I guess, to callous makers of pillows and quilted vests.

Well, little Amy saves the flock. She leads them down the whole Atlantic flyway, piloting a peculiar ultra-light plane— small, gray, and goose-shaped.

Montessori kids who'd seen that movie, I guessed, would think all geese are as lovable as Amy's. And what then, if they glanced out of the school windows and saw Arrie and me bridling birds and hauling them up to my truck? They might storm down the hill, yelling, attacking with crayons, pelting us with play-doh…

By the time Arrie and I pulled into the school grounds that gray afternoon, we'd planned just to reconnoiter. But, to our surprise, there were the five geese, hunkered down on the creek's bank, just back from a raid or plotting one.

Without a plan, I got out and circled slowly behind them, just to check their reaction. It was too good to hope for. They stood up, honking, and headed south along the bank, toward a large play area surrounded by snow fence. As I followed, I moved slightly to the right to steer them left. As if in close-order drill, the geese wheeled in that direction and waddled straight through the fence's wide gateway.

By now Arrie was out of the truck, climbing down the hill to take charge.

"We got to block this opening," he said. "I'll stay here and keep them in. You get home and bring back some fencing and wire—and some rope for halters." I left him standing in light rain and jumped in the truck.

Halfway up Bissell Road, the skies spilled out a deluge. I imagined Arrie, soaked and stoic, but drove on. In fifteen minutes I was back. By the snow fence, old Arrie stood pillar-like in the downpour, holding a plastic trash can lid over his head. You don't last to eighty-two without being resourceful.

We fenced the gap, corralled the geese in one corner, and managed to halter three of them. The other two opened five-foot wingspreads, cleared the fence and landed in the middle of the creek, honking goose curses back at us.

With wary eyes on the school windows, we led three blustering captives up to the truck. Luck held and we weren't spotted. Maybe we'll try for the others another day.

All that was several weeks ago. The three geese are now alone in my new sheep yard. This winter they'll share shed and yard with my three ewes, who are off in Oaksville now, consorting with a ram. Arrie says sheep and geese get along. I hope so, but those birds seem awfully bossy…

❖ ❖ ❖

Someone should've warned me. I should have known what might be coming. I suppose, though, there was a warning of sorts. A week before Christmas, Anne was up from Annapolis. It was cold weather, blustery. She and I were inside Schneider's Bakery in Cooperstown, sitting over cups of coffee. Between serving her customers, Chris Lord called over to us, "Any big holiday plans?"

"Well," I said, "we've got a guest coming, and we're going to cook a goose." At that, a woman sitting at the other table turned toward us, laughing.

"Good luck!" she said.

"You've cooked one?" I asked.

"Not for ten years," she said, "and never again!" She followed with a horror story about hours of plucking; about choking, drifting clouds of goose down; and finally, for the whole roasting time of the bird, about bailing buckets of hot goose grease out of the pan.

I wasn't put off, though. I had a solution, both for the plucking and the grease problem. I'd skin my goose.

It wasn't that hard. First I dropped one of the three big birds with the twenty-two, and, after a detour by the chopping block, took it into the barn. Then followed about forty minutes of loosening, pulling, pushing, tugging—a bit like getting a sullen kid out of a snowsuit. At the end, I had the feathered pelt off, and stuck to its inside was a good half inch of goose fat. Left behind was a wine-colored carcass, about seven pounds. It was beautiful: Unlike the chunkiness of a chicken's, this carcass had an ocean liner's proportions—high, narrow, and long.

When our friend Greg Byrer arrived from Maine, the three of us prepared our goose dinner, all agreeing that it's Dickens' *A Christmas Carol* that makes a holiday goose seem so apt. With the Mormon Choir resounding through the house, Anne made a beautiful dressing of bread crumbs, chopped prunes and onion, dried apple and spinach. Greg flavored a winter squash casserole with brown sugar, butter, chopped pecans, and a good dollop of Meyer's rum. With some pride, I trussed my fat-free goose and set it on a rack in a roaster, adding red wine before I covered it.

Into a slow oven it went, to cook, according to the recipe, for two and a half hours. I checked it periodically. All seemed well, except the bird developed a sharp list to starboard. But it smelled ambrosial and seemed to be cooking just fine.

On an antique Blue Willow platter, that goose made a handsome centerpiece, surrounded on the white tablecloth by bowls of winter squash, green beans almondine, heaped dressing, and lots of condiments. Wine glasses and silverware gleamed in the candlelight as we sat down to a feast. I felt as suffused by the season as Bob Cratchit himself.

But when I started to carve, I was carried back to Cub Scouts—to slicing balsa wood for building models. For, despite the tight cover and all the red wine, this bird was dry. Dry? It was damned near mummified. Without comment, I sawed away, laying truly beautiful slices onto our three plates. When everyone was served and we'd drunk a toast to the season, we cut into the slices and raised the first bites to our lips.

It was the most labored chewing since Chaplin's "Little Tramp," starving, had to boil and eat his boots. Greg, always kind, finally spoke. "The flavor is really very good…" And dear Anne added a positive spin, saying brightly, "I think you've invented goose jerky."

No one asked for seconds. We made a meal of dressing, winter squash, and green beans.

What went wrong? Did I cook the goose too long? Should I have laid bacon strips across its back since, ironically, I'd turned it into such lean meat? Or was that just a tough old goose, good only for the soup pot? If readers have suggestions—based on experience, mind you—I'd welcome them.

Whatever the cause, I know memories of this year's bird debacle will always raise Tiny Tim's delighted cry: "There never was such a goose!"

◆ ◆ ◆

Six months later, a great quiet has settled over the barnyard. In part that's because both sheep and calves are in Arrie Hecox's pasture for the summer; they do their respective baaing and mooing down there. I visit them regularly, scratch heads all around, and listen to any complaints about bedding or food. Then, like the adept administrator I used to be, I nod and tell them I'll certainly look into the matter. And then I go home.

Back at my place, there are almost no noisemakers except the chickens. The hens do their share of cackling, and the rooster still sounds a salute about four-thirty each morning.

He also crows randomly during the day, when there's need to affirm who's in charge. But generally he's a temperate bird, and he governs more by indirection than force. I admire that. He's my kind of manager.

What's really made for the eerie calm is the silence of the geese. My botched try at making one of them into Christmas dinner still left two geese who, despite the sheep's meek example, remained messy, loud, and demanding. And very touchy, too, about anyone who upset their perverse idea of order. My walking into sight fell into that category. I couldn't step onto the back porch, fifty yards away, without one of them spotting me from beyond the fence behind the barn. At once he'd call the other one. Then, together, necks stretched and bills straight up, they'd shriek and honk insults at me— in unmusical, clashing pitches. The effect was not something easily ignored.

What a pleasure, then, to open the *Pennysaver* a couple of weeks ago and read an ad in the Farm Column: "Wanted," it said. "Nasty goose. The meaner the better." I grabbed the telephone.

It was answered by a farmer living at the far reaches of our *Pennysaver*'s range—to the north and east, on toward Albany. The farmer explained that he has a new neighbor, city-bred, one who has no sense of what a property line is. Or maybe he does, since he'd been dumping his trash on the wrong side of it. The farmer wanted a mean goose for guard duty, one that would sound the alarm when incursions occurred and borders were breached.

"I've got the goose for you," I told him. "Better yet, I've got two." I told him about my Brookwood rejects—about their vile dispositions, about the uproar they raise when they sense any intrusion. Over the phone, we arranged a trade: two laying hens for a brace of mean geese. A few days later I had the chickens, and the geese were forty miles away, doing the work they were born for—search and destroy.

83

So it's a good deal quieter here now—only the wild birds' songs, the rooster's occasional crow, the cackle of a laying hen especially pleased with herself. I can now go onto the screened porch, iced tea and book in hand, without suffering indignities from my own poultry.

And in making his rounds, Owen the cat now feels safe in cutting across the fenced barnyard. He doesn't mind threading his way among clucking chickens, but he'd no more have turned his back on those geese than I would. That cat's no dummy.

19

Old Stones Settle

I pass them on one of my regular walks and sometimes stop, lean on the fence rail, and see what they have to say. They've been lying right there, husband and wife, for almost two hundred years; but they continue to speak. Each of their graves, right at the front of the Adams family cemetery on Route 26, has a tall, round-topped slab; and each slab carries a poem. As I walk the mile back to my house, I often think of one poem or the other. I'll tell you about his first.

He was a Fly Creek Valley pioneer: John Adams brought his family west in 1790. When he died, in 1810 at age sixty-seven, carved messages on tombstones were much the custom. Grieving farewells, pious testaments, elaborate eulogies—in cemeteries all around here, examples in verse abound. They are flanked by carved weeping willows, veiled urns, and angels bowed in grief. The undertakers and stone carvers of that time had sample books to choose from. One scanned the books, I suppose, as one does the greeting card racks today, looking for just the right verse.

John Adams' epitaph is a message to us. It continues his voice on earth, at least until the elements finally erase the fading words. Written in the first person, his poem is a grim admonition:

> *"Here contemplate while passing by:*
> *As you are now, so once was I:*
> *As I am now, so you must be*
> *Prepare for death and follow me."*

That much is standard stuff, and certainly open to a pious reading. But, walking back home, I often think about two final lines:

> *"This silent grave, alas how small,*
> *A spot of earth is now my all."*

Heading home, I wonder first, who chose that text. Did John Adams' widow, sitting in a dim parlor, a sample book open on her lap? If so, what made her decide, "That one. That sounds like John"?

Did she see irony in "spot of earth," and "alas how small"? Was her John perhaps like the scriptural rich farmer, who'd planned excitedly to pull down his barns and build greater ones for all his goods—and then abruptly died? Was it a land-hungry man who'd brought her to the wilderness twenty years before, one who'd thought of little else—one who'd bitterly resent ending with a mere "spot of earth"?

But, then, maybe John Adams himself chose that inscription. Surely he had picked that prominent plot, right at the edge of the road. Why not leave a message in stone, one that walkers from Toddsville to Fly Creek would surely read? Why not lecture the living from the grave?

But if he had chosen to lecture, what was his theme? Perhaps, "Prepare for a good death." Perhaps. But the tone's all wrong, isn't it? The voice in those chiseled words is sober and stern, yes. But the tone is darker yet...

One evening, almost back home, I grasped it. It's that word "alas." A pious voice would surely have no use for "alas"—much less for saying a narrow grave is "now my all." This voice, speaking beyond death, doesn't address us from the Great Beyond.

It speaks from beneath the compacted earth.

Someone, wife or husband, by chance or intent, chose a message that sounds bleak, embittered, even profane. All right, that may only be the end of the twentieth century misreading the early nineteenth. And since I'm often unsure of my own, much less others' intentions, how dare I surmise about the long dead?

Still, as I head on toward my own home, I can't help but wonder about it.

◆ ◆ ◆

Dear God, who'd inflict such a name on a child?

I thought that when I first saw the epitaph, "Mrs. Submit Adams, Consort of Mr. John Adams."

She outlived John Adams by three years. Her stone carries a far gentler poem—picked, one imagines, by her daughter Sarah, who married Simeon Clinton and lived close by:

"Her hands while here her alms bestowed,
Her glory's future harvest sow'd.
The sweet remembrance of the just
Like a green root renews and bears
A train of blessings for her heirs,
When dying nature sleeps in dust."

Returned to the earth, but living on in glory. A good woman, remembered with love. I'm glad of it.

But that name. "Submit!"

She'd been born in New England in 1743, at a time when naming girls for virtues was falling out of fashion. Three generations before, even two, such names were common; a girls' Sunday School roster would have sounded like a morality-play cast: Faith, Prudence, Hope, Charity, Temperance, Purity, Patience…

But wait. Unlike those names, this one isn't an abstract noun. It's a verb—in the imperative mode. This poor girl's name was a command, and it must have sounded like one, every time she was addressed.

"Submit, set the table." "Submit, go to the chalkboard." "Submit, stop talking!" "Submit!"

Submit.

Where did that name, that verb, come from? Ephesians, I think, Chapter Five: "Wives, submit yourselves unto your own husbands, as unto the Lord…" Some latter-day Puritan (her father—I can't imagine her mother doing it) chose the name to set the pattern of her life.

If that was his attitude, what must her childhood have been? Was she schooled to meekness? Was she a girl of downcast eyes, bowed in spirit, even in body?

Then she was married to John Adams, whose stern and (at least to me) haughty words still confront readers from his tombstone. How did Submit fare with him, I wonder, through more than forty years of marriage?

As I said, she outlived him by three years. And then someone picked a stone for her identical in shape to her husband's. But old stones settle, and hers now stands about four inches taller than his.

That pleases me.

20

Natty Bumppo Slept Here...

Something intriguing appears in the *1878 History of Otsego County*. The book says that the prototype for Fenimore Cooper's Natty Bumppo was an old man who wandered in and out of Cooperstown during Cooper's youth. The man's name was David Shipman, and he lived three miles out of the village on the east bank of Oaks Creek, about halfway between Toddsville and Fly Creek hamlet. That puts his cabin about where Oaks Creek and Fly Creek converge, just above today's Fork Shop Road.

And it means that the original Leatherstocking lived his later years not a mile from my house, which was already standing in those days. Of course I like to imagine the rough-cut old recluse standing in my dooryard, drinking from a tin dipper; or perhaps inside on a bleak November day, warming by the fireside. It'd be stretching it to say, "Natty Bumppo slept here"—but, who knows? Maybe a late March nor'easter, sweeping in a wall of snow on blizzard winds, blocked him from getting home one evening. Maybe old Bumppo spent a night snoring by my hearth, scenting the air with the deer-skin he wore and (given his likely hygiene) with his own hide.

But the History adds another detail, one Cooper chose to ignore. For a time Bumppo, i.e., Shipman, had a wife sharing the cabin where the creeks join. She died well before David, and he brought a Baptist minister from Hartwick to bury her close by their home.

The minister was outraged by the site David had chosen. It was boggy land (still is), and as the grave was dug, it half filled with water. Shipman was adamant; she must be buried by their home. "And if I live to die," the book quotes him, "I expect to be buried there myself."

It's Shipman's "if" that stops you. Most all of us, after all, manage to live long enough to die. But for David Shipman, it seems to have been possibility rather than certainty. That's disarming. Even endearing.

Well, David did live long enough to die, though it happened many years later. But, sad to say, they didn't lay him to rest beside his wife. The *1878 History* says he was buried in the Adams cemetery, which now fronts on Route 26. But by 1878, his exact place in the cemetery had already been lost, forgotten.

I think of the original Bumppo as often as I walk past that

cemetery. And when I hike through the wet stretches where Oaks Creek and Fly Creek converge, I think of his missus, given a sea burial, though a good ways inland from any coast. She was left there in another now-lost grave to carry on her long voyage alone.

Leatherstocking wouldn't have wanted that. I'm sure of it.

21

With Hands on Hearts

A remarkable man died a few years ago at a nursing home in upstate New York. I went to his memorial service there. The large room was filled with family and friends from Edmeston, his nearby hometown. No one was there merely out of social obligation. This gentle man had touched many, had been deeply loved. As a half-dozen speakers reminisced about the man's place in their lives, there were smiles, tears, a deep sense of shared affection.

But few knew his first name. David Rosenberg, who died at sixty-two, was largely known simply as "Brother." It was the most apt of nicknames.

Born with Down's syndrome, Brother Rosenberg initially came to Edmeston, New York, as a resident of the Otsego School, predecessor of today's renowned Pathfinder Village. In short order, though, he'd been unofficially adopted into the family that ran the school, the Chesebroughs. For almost all his life he shared their home, a brother to their five children as they grew toward adulthood. And Brother grew up with them, into his own kind of maturity—one that always carried a child's joy in imagination, a child's sense of fun.

One of his eulogists was John Blackman, Edmeston's retired Baptist pastor. John drew nods and laughter from all as he recalled Brother as an early ecumenist. One Christmas, perhaps twenty-five years before, the Otsego School nativity pageant was performed in the church. Brother was cast as a shepherd, dressed in his bathrobe and a bath towel burnoose.

After he'd knelt at the manger and had turned toward the

congregation to leave the stage, he was inspired to improvise. Something was needed, he must have thought, to intensify the moment. So Brother Rosenberg, son of Abraham, gave the Baptists a warm smile and piously crossed himself.

Prudy Chesebrough Whitehead spoke for the family at the memorial service; and she, too, stressed Brother's ability to read the moment and respond to it. Never more so, Prudy said, than when she and her brothers and sisters lost their grandmother.

Lib Lockerbie had served as Brother's surrogate grandmother, and a special closeness linked them. When she died, the Chesebroughs were unsure how they'd comfort Brother, who'd never encountered death. They decided to take him to Lib's home after calling hours, so he could see her at rest.

The family walked Brother into the very familiar living room and crossed it to the strange box. While Brother stared at his dear friend, John and Anna Clare Chesebrough tried to explain what had happened. Then they fell silent. Perhaps Brother understood their explanation; without question, he read the feeling in the room. Here people were standing together, solemnly attentive. How should he react?

He searched his limited past experience for a parallel and came up with only one: a baseball crowd, standing in shared solemnity for the National Anthem. And so, at attention by the casket, Brother placed hand over heart. He sang "The Star-

Spangled Banner." He was tone-deaf, and the words were a bit impressionistic. But it was his best tribute to his friend. A perfect tribute.

As Prudy finished speaking, she and everyone present wept for a good man gone.

But, one might say, Brother was shadowed by Down Syndrome all his days. Could you call Brother's life a complete, a successful one?

Dear Lord, yes!

But his intelligence was sharply limited—

Well, whose isn't? Just maybe, if we could contrast our scant knowledge with the vast unknowable beyond us, the difference between Brother's capacity and that of the brightest human would seem too small to note, much less stress. That's the case, surely, in God's eyes.

Brother Rosenberg excelled, not in intellect, but in goodness and warmth. Those were his rich gifts. Very often I saw him read someone's sadness (sometimes mine), squint up with deep concern, and place a hand on the person's arm.

"Be happy," he'd say. The words were half plea, half command. And the touch transmitted more than concern. Most often, it seemed to heal.

When all the speakers were done and Brother's memorial service had ended with a benediction, everyone remained standing. It was then we paid our best tribute to our friend. He'd have loved it.

We all sang "The Star-Spangled Banner." With hands over hearts.

22

Mary's Little Lambs— and Maude's and Maggie's

y three ewes are big as barrels. With splayed sides and matchstick legs, each of them now resembles a broad kerosene tank cradled on a pipe rack. Their romps with the ram were back in November, so lambs should come in mid-March. I don't see how these ewes are going to hold out that long. I'm brand-new at this, but it looks to me like lambs could show up any day now—or, more likely, any night.

I've been reading *Raising Sheep the Modern Way*. In fact, I study it. Obsessively. The book says that moving the ewes' feeding to mid-morning will make them much more likely to deliver during the day—rather than, as I imagine, at 3 A.M., at ten below, in a snowstorm, with forty-mile gusts shaking the sheep shed, rattling its windows and me.

The book also says, soothingly, that ewes do the whole job of delivery themselves in eighty percent of the cases. But then for pages it amplifies on that other twenty-percent, describing all the things that can go wrong and what must be done to remedy them.

In the eighty-percent, a little lamb enters the world like a diver into a pool: front legs straight out, head down and between them. Other lambs, however, perhaps caught off-guard by the eviction notice, head out like a swimmer in mid-stroke, one leg forward, one trailing back. The trailing leg means the shoulder can wedge. Worse is the lamb that starts its dive with head turned, looking wistfully back over its shoulder. And still worse is twin lambs taking the plunge at once— a tangle of legs and hoofs and heads that must be sorted, with

one lamb encouraged to go back and wait its turn.

Twins, my books says, are common. (Two of my ewes, mine for less than a year, have a history of twinning.) And triplets are not unusual. Whence comes my worst nightmare: All three ewes, all carrying triplets, starting their labor at once; all three having complications—and, of course, all in the middle of that wild, sub-zero, three A.M. snowstorm.

My own minimal knowledge of obstetrics has come mostly from movie dialog. ("Boil lots of water! And tear up some sheets!") Beyond that, I'm as green as Prissy about "birthin' babies"—of any species. *Raising Sheep* is a help here. Besides instructions and warnings, it gives a check-list of supplies and equipment to have on hand when the time comes.

The list runs to three dozen items—towels, heat lamp, hair dryer, scissors, iodine, lubricant, antiseptic ointment, etc. It calls for a "set of cords, sterilized," to be used if two lambs are heading out at once. You must snag the hoofs of the one that you push to the back of the line, so you can draw it forward again when its turn comes. (Pushing the lamb back brings Billy Crystal to mind: In *City Slickers,* you'll remember, he lost his Rolex inside a cow.)

I've searched that long list vainly for "small flask of Jim Beam." They also left out "iron resolve" and "nerves of steel."

But, mind you, I'm not attempting this just "by the book." Better, far more immediate help is close at hand. Standing behind me—and available by phone and also in person—is the entire generous membership of The Leatherstocking Sheep Association.

I may be calling on them.

23

Pigs—the Last Act

*W*ell, what was pigs has become pork. Last Sunday morning found the pen empty and quiet. In the chilly garage sat three broad tin washtubs of ribs, roasts, and chops. Two more held hams, hocks, and bacon for smoking. Another was full of scraps for sausage.

The day before had been a perfect one for the job: low thirties, fairly still, and only light flurries. I was out back at five, and Anne, up from Annapolis to help, was there soon after. Under a big basswood tree out back, we'd set a steel drum on four cinder blocks, with split wood stacked nearby. Next to the barrel, tall sawhorses and an old door formed a table. Anne and I arranged the tools on the table, hauled twelve buckets of hot water from the house, got the fire going. Then we placed a big pot of coffee and a plate of doughnuts on the back porch.

At eight-thirty the water was seething, and a team of my old friends had gathered around the coffee and doughnuts. John Chesebrough had come from Edmeston, and Howard Talbot from Cooperstown. Frank Famulare was down from Manlius; one of the two pigs belonged to his mother and sister. Arrie Hecox drove over from his place, and Dr. Bob Mackie had come down the valley to help, and perhaps in case we did damage to ourselves. (Through the day, a dozen other friends were in and out of the yard, to offer encouragement or shake their heads over the bunch of us.)

Recently I'd heard many descriptions of how "the old timers" did this ritual about to begin. Usually it involved a lot of hard cider—anesthesia against the cold and the grimmer elements of the job. The old stories usually described befuddled men staggering and falling in the snow, lying on their backs in helpless laughter. One story described a toper who, benumbed, stood too close to the kettle and worked away with one pantleg smoldering. After hearing about the traditional ritual, I settled for the revised standard version. All the essentials remained, but the cider played a very small role. Late in the morning Anne came out of the house with a tray, and we drank a modest toast from small paper cups.

The first and most sobering part of the job went quickly and, I think, without pain. First a shot from the .22, then a quick knife thrust into the throat. The shot felled the pig instantly, and blood drained from the body in minutes. Not a squeak, not a squeal.

The mood lightened as we all hauled on a rope and drew a first heavy carcass out of the pen, stumbling up a snowy slope and toward my house. Then came more hauling as the first was hung from a long basswood limb, lowered into the scalding water, then hoisted out and swung onto the trestle table. After that, much hard work, scraping off the bristles.

And when the carcass was smooth, still more hauling. Using another tackle farther down the limb, we raised the pig from the table, hind legs first, and hung it over a wheelbarrow for gutting. John and Frank, who had never met before, worked as if trained as a team, stripping out offal, salvaging the liver and other edible parts. The rest of us helped as we could, and all joined in to brace the carcass as John stood on a ladder to saw it in half, down the length of the backbone.

When the two halves had been hung to cool in the garage, we broke for lunch. Then it was back to the yard and the whole process again for the second pig. It all went well. By four o'clock I was alone in the yard, taking down the tackle and dousing the fire.

What's stayed with me from that day? First, the shared sense of soberness as the slaughtering was done. Life was ending, life of special intensity. A live pig blazes with a greedy, fierce vitality—snorting, shoving, squealing, biting at anything that blocks its way to food. With that gone, a pig in death is a profound contrast.

And then, in the next phase, I recall the excitement of teamwork outside in the bracing cold; hard, useful work, but undertaken with a sense of play—and a sense of shared danger, too, from fire, scalding water, heavy weights, sharp blades. And I recall my pleasure in watching experienced men apply special skills, and in learning as I watched. And then, my own weary stiffness at the end of the clean-up. And my feeling of finality, accomplishment.

I recall the gang of my good friends scraping away together on the hide, wreathed in snow flurries and wind-blown smoke. Wiping their eyes and noses. Laughing heartily at one another's jokes.

And, of course, I think of those pigs relaxed in death. So still against the snow. So suddenly dignified.

Oh, and I recall a last touch from the old traditions: Lunch was held at Peg Famulare's house; Anne had taken the first pig's liver there ahead of us. Peg fried some, and we shared it as a part of the meal around her kitchen table.

It was delicious. We praised it to one another. And were grateful.

24

"The Diviltries of the Law"

A while back, I told you about the crusty old trapper who very likely inspired James Fenimore Cooper's most famous literary character, Natty Bumppo. The real man was David Shipman, and he was a well-known Cooperstown figure during the author's boyhood.

Well, now I have more of the story to tell you, courtesy of Fred Powers of Hinman Hollow. (Fred's got a bit of Bumppo in him, I think. He and his wife are building a log cabin in the Hollow—building slowly, Fred stressed. At four score years and more, Fred says it takes him about a week to do a good day's work.)

Fred told me my writing about David Shipman recalled a story that he'd heard as a boy—a while back, mind you, when World War I was still called The Great War. Fred remembered hearing that Shipman, as a very old man, was brought to trial for killing an Indian. Standing on the bank of Oaks Creek, he had shot the Indian out of his canoe.

Old David Shipman, the story went, was acquitted. The jury accepted his claim that the Indian, a known malefactor, had been harassing him, threatening his life.

Fred's story makes an interesting parallel to something Cooper melded into *The Pioneers,* his fictional account of Cooperstown's founding. Toward the book's end, he has old Natty Bumppo brought up before the court on charges of killing a deer a few days before the season opened, and of resisting arrest.

Bumppo is angered and grieved. He'd lived by hunting

deer for forty years, long before the town and the order of law appeared. In the log courtroom, he boldly challenges Squire Templeton (modeled on Cooper's own land-baron father), who is acting as judge.

"You've driven God's creatur's [sic] from the wilderness, where his providence had put them for his own pleasure; and you've brought in the troubles and diviltries of the law, where no man was ever known to disturb another."

It's the classic clash of the American frontier, isn't it? The first to arrive, the pioneers, live simply by their own law. Then population gradually begins to increase. And then appears Rousseau's "social contract," offering the benefits of organized society but limiting individual's unchecked freedom—and enforcing limits with threats of punishment.

Writing in the year 1823, Cooper seems to have looked back at David Shipman as much more than an odd old man dressed in buckskin and living by his gun and his dogs. As Cooper began to originate the myth of the American frontier, he must have seen Shipman, transmuted into Bumppo, as the perfect emblem of the frontiersmen's courage and their pain as an organized society supplanted their way of life—and them as well.

The boy Cooper would surely have attended Shipman's trial; outside church and the taverns, the courts provided early settlements with their best entertainment. And perhaps it was the memory of Shipman tried for murder because the old man had protected his own life in the old, pre-civilized way, that made Bumppo come to focus in Cooper's mind as centerpiece for all the *Leatherstocking Tales.*

For, having first created Bumppo as an elderly man in *The Pioneers,* Cooper later wrote him a young manhood and a full maturity in *The Last of the Mohicans, The Pathfinder,* and *The Deerslayer.*

Anyway, I'll bet you're also grateful to Fred Powers for adding to the story. He's certainly changed the way I look at Oaks Creek.

When I've walked across the Fork Shop iron bridge, I've often looked upstream and imagined Shipman's cabin there, set back on the east bank. Now Fred's got me seeing more.

There's an overturned canoe, birchbark, drifting downstream toward me. And, face down in the shallows, a sprawled figure, buckskin clothes soaked black by the water.

And, standing in a half crouch on the bank, a frail old man who clenches a smoking flintlock. The rage that had twisted his face is slacking off, giving place to anguish.

Next time you pass there, stop to look. You'll see them, too.

◆ ◆ ◆

It's odd how one of these columns leads to another. Just after I put Fred Powers' story in a column, I had a call from

Dr. Bob Mackie. Had I ever heard, he asked, of another famous early Cooperstown trial—one that ended with a man hanged and spectators nursing bruises and broken limbs?

Bob's story was a new one to me, and intriguing, too. So I began asking around among my older Fly Creek friends. Sure enough, they'd all heard the story, but with some variations. A constant element, though, was the great crowd and the injuries many suffered. Then a friend passed on a written account of the incident. It's so good (and, in a way, so haunting) that I have to share it with you.

The account is in *Todds Ville, Recollections of an Early Mill Town,* a fine booklet compiled in 1974 by Lawrence Gardner. Mr. Gardner includes the story of the hanging, as written by Cuyler Carr and originally published in a 1926 issue of *The Freeman's Journal.*

Mr. Carr, now long dead, had a unique perspective on the hanging: The executed man, Levi Kelley, was husband to his great-aunt.

Kelley was a gifted millwright who designed and built many of Oaks Creek's early mills. Tragically, he had a temper as keen as his mechanical skills, but nowhere near so well controlled.

"In a fit of anger," writes Mr. Carr, "he would throw at a fellow workman any tool he might have in his hand or within his reach." So harsh a man was he that his abused young wife fled to her family home and never returned. Levi lived on, alone, on the Pierstown farm that had been their home.

When he leased the use of the farm to a tenant in 1827, Kelley's wrath found a new object. In his eyes, poor Abram Spafard could do nothing right. Levi ranted to his neighbors that he'd put a ball through Spafard before cold weather.

And he did just that. In September 1827, enraged over where Spafard had stored a load of oats, Levi Kelley burst into Spafard's kitchen and shot him dead in front of his wife. She was left a widow with seven small children.

Jailed in Cooperstown, Kelley was visited there by a neighbor. Cuyler Carr recounts that, on departing, the neighbor tried to comfort him:

"I hope you will receive justice."

Kelley's bitter reply: "That is what I am afraid of."

And justice is what he received. He was tried, found guilty, condemned to death. His hanging, scheduled for three days after Christmas, drew a huge crowd in holiday spirits. Little grimness among these people; a murderer was about to get his due. They would see both wickedness punished and an object lesson for the living.

For in 1827, a hanging was a celebration of the common good, of society rising up to protect itself. So, excited, muffled with scarves and furs against winter cold, the spectators crowded into the rickety temporary stands. They hunched their shoulders, puffed out clouds of vapor, perhaps stamped their numbed feet.

And then—the rifle-crack of snapping boards, screams, shouts of fear and pain. People had been pitched over backward and were struggling to sit up in the snowy ruins. Moans and sobbing. Calls for help.

Standing on the gallows trapdoor, Levi Kelley heard all this, writes Mr. Carr.

"The murderer, hearing the noise, inquired of the sheriff the cause and when told of the accident said, 'I'm sorry.' The black cap was adjusted, the rope tightened, trap sprung and Levi Kelley went to meet his Creator."

"I'm sorry," he had said. Not, it seems, for savageness towards his fellows, cruel abuse of his wife, murder of a young husband and father. But sorry for the accident—for pain he didn't cause, but simply occasioned.

I wonder, when that rope snapped taut a hundred and sixty-eight years ago, what sort of mind was it that exploded into scarlet, then black?

25

Serving Up Food, and Friendship, Too

A few weeks ago I drove the ten miles to Hartwick through driving rain. Riding shotgun with me was Barry Rumple, a good friend from up Cemetery Road. In the back of the truck, under cover, was a handsome, heavy bench of treated lumber. Barry, an octogenarian, had built the bench as a tribute to his dear friends Richard and Corinne Pollak. Richard died last year, and the bench is intended for the Hartwick Cemetery, so that Corinne can sit near Richard and reminisce about the life they shared.

And what a life it was! Richard started out with high hopes of being a professional singer. He was gifted with quick wit and a magnificent tenor; and in the early nineteen-fifties, he had headed for New York City and a career on the stage.

It was not to be. Despite an agent's best efforts, there were just no jobs—except one. NBC television wanted to boost the success of its still-new show, "Howdy Doody," by hiring a half-dozen clones for one of its popular characters: Clarabell the Clown. The secondary Clarabells (each billed as the-one-and-only) would tour the country, visiting schools and hospitals—and, as you'd expect, shoe stores, to help advertise the show's sponsor, Poll Parrot Shoes. Ironically, Richard Pollak, the man with the grand tenor, was hired as a Clarabell—a clown who had no voice.

The on-camera Clarabell was a gleeful anarchist. His seltzer-bottle antics upset Buffalo Bob and the other cast members—but convulsed the Peanut Gallery, all of them delighted by a big person acting like a kid out of control. By contrast, the traveling Clarabells were to project warmth, gentleness, and good will. According to Corinne, Richard had harrowing stories of wildly excited kids, conditioned by the TV Clarabell, mobbing him and trying to goad him into the mischief they'd seen on the screen. "Sometimes I had to back into a corner," Richard used to say, "just to protect myself from kidney punches!"

Richard's Clarabell work lasted only about three years, long enough for him to decide against a career on the road. Not long after, he and Corinne discovered what was to be

their life's work together. Settling outside Hartwick, they opened "The Country Kitchen," a friendly, informal restaurant that became second home for many, many people. The aspiring stage soloist became the singing cook, entertaining customers with music and jokes. And warm-hearted Corinne became hostess and foil, carrying trays and trading patter with Richard at the grill. People loved it and came back, again and again.

And not just locals. In the eighties, Corinne's regular *The Freeman's Journal* column, "What's Cookin' in Hartwick?" was picked up by *Grit,* a nationwide family newspaper, and renamed "Letter from Hartwick." The editors—and readers— loved her homey accounts of the musical restaurant and of village life in Hartwick.

"I thought they'd just put my stuff in a regional edition," says Corinne, "but pretty soon I started getting letters from all over the country—and from Canada, and abroad! And then we started getting readers as customers. They'd be on vacation and drive out of their way to eat with us, hear Richard's songs and jokes, join in the sing-alongs..."

Then, two years ago, Richard was diagnosed with Lou Gehrig's disease. In time, it took away his song, his virtuoso whistling, his speech. Then the disease worsened, and the much-loved restaurant had to be closed. And too soon, the silent clown of three decades before, silenced himself at the end, was gone.

As rain fell steadily outside the fogged windows, Barry and I visited with Corinne in the closed restaurant—still set up with place mats, glasses, and flatware.

"We always thought of this as our dining room," she said, looking around—"just a little bigger than most people's. I guess that's why they felt at home here."

People did, and for good reason. She and Richard had spent a shared life offering guests, not just good food, but also unaffected human warmth. And though Richard was never a stage professional, he—and Corinne—performed beautifully all those years. What the two of them did together made many people very happy.

That's a fine thing for Corinne to sit quietly on Barry's bench and recall.

26

Two Sheep Tales

I spent a recent morning on the screened porch with a long-overdue visitor—rain. Sight of it, and its sound and smell, exulted me. The rain was easing the drought that has dwarfed corn and left fields and gardens brittle, ruined. If the scorched meadows had senses, that rain would have felt like balm spread on burns.

I sat with a book and glanced up randomly to admire my red barn, dark with wetness; and beyond it, the woods, rejoicing with wet leaves and branches. Closer at hand, a big puddle graced the driveway, bright surface rough with raindrops. Even with my eyes down on a page, I heard the steady drumming, the gargle in the downspouts; and I smelled the wet earth. It all seemed holy. It felt like church out there on the back porch.

The book I held came through the mail some months ago: *A Shepherd Looks at Psalm 23*. I'd had my own copy of the book back in the nineteen-seventies, long before I'd ever met a sheep. Phyllis Petri had sent this copy to me from Hartwick Seminary. Phyllis wrote that her mother had recently died, and she was dispersing a number of her things—especially her books, since such books should always be shared. Well said, Phyllis. And thank you.

Anyway, since I often write about my small flock, Phyllis thought I'd like the sheep book. I do, and understand it ever so much better now.

Because its lay-preacher author, Philip Keller, raised sheep for many years, he sees the psalm's image of God as shepherd, and humans as sheep, with clear eyes—no pious sentiment. One of his major points is that it's no compliment to be called sheep.

Sheep, who can be disarmingly charming, are also dirty, dim, strong-willed beasts, who often seem bent on their own destruction. They will walk past clean water to drink from a foul pool, and are notorious for rushing off after any seeming leader. If one sheep gets separated from the flock and becomes "cast," (i.e. rolls on its back and can't get up), it will smother in hours unless the shepherd seeks it out and sets it back on its feet.

It's apt, says Keller wryly, that the Almighty has chosen to call us sheep: "The behavior of sheep and human beings is similar in many ways..." He continues, "Our mass mind... our fears and timidity, our stubbornness and stupidity, our perverse habits are all parallels of profound importance."

A good shepherd, he infers, is devoted to the sheep, not only because of some qualities, but in spite of others. (That rings true, doesn't it? It applies to love of all kinds.)

The awful drought, though now tempered by some rain, has burnt out my sheep's pasture. The standing grass is so empty of nourishment that the flock bunches at the fence at sight of me, baaing piteously, begging for baled hay. Hay, mind you, that I'd laid in for cold weather. I hadn't planned on their needing it till late September.

But I have no green pastures in which they can feed and lie down. And so I haul out a still-fresh bale, cut the twine, shake bats of hay loose over the fence. The sheep smell the hay before I even break the bale, and they shoulder one another for position. As they attack the hay, all baaing stops. Each grabs a great swatch and then stands chewing noisily, looking up at me. Sometimes Maggie, her mouth full, tries to give an appreciative baa.

"Mooof," she says.

"Good animals," I say, pleased at their zest for what's been given. I like to provide—hay or water, medicine or shelter, hoof-trimming or help with lambing. It's good to be needed.

On the porch, watching the blessed rain, I think that one must try to be a good shepherd. And, I guess, try to be a good sheep, too.

◆ ◆ ◆

Tom Deason deserves a medal, for "Courage Under Fire," or "Service Above and Beyond Duty." An amiable Canadian, Tom's a World War II vet with a bulldog look but eyes bright with good humor. He's engaged to Anne's cousin Joan; and the two visited in Fly Creek recently while heading home from Florida.

Anne and Joan are as close as sisters; and, to my great delight, Tom Deason is a truly gifted storyteller. He and I knocked back some fine Canadian rye as Tom laid out tales from a long, interesting life: about being swept up in giddy celebrations as WWII ended, about a young man's adventures in the wilds of western Canada, about his many years as a press-room compositor for two big daily papers in Toronto.

Tom and Joan were with us just after lambing time. Most of the related jobs were already done, except for docking the last-born lamb's tail. Lambs, you probably know, are born with long tails that dangle almost to their heels. The tails become soiled and, when wagged, toss unpleasant stuff onto the animals' backs—and into the valuable fleece. The solution is simple. Within days of the lamb's birth, put a thick rubber band on the tail, about three inches out from the body. It's painless and it works: In two weeks or three, the atrophied tail just drops off.

I actually saw this happen last year. Four lambs had been gamboling in the sunshine, racing around and sometimes bouncing straight into the air, as if each animal was mounted on four pogo sticks. One playful ram ran into the shed and then vaulted out again, over the stoop. When he landed solidly on all four feet, his tail fell off.

The lamb froze and did a literal double take, looking twice back over his shoulder. Then he circled the former attachment, sniffing it. And then he walked off slowly, uneasily. I guess he thought another jolt might cost him another part.

Putting that heavy band on the tail, by the way, isn't hard with the right tool. It's called an "elastrator." As the name suggests, it can bind off more than tails. I won't say more. The thought makes my stomach muscles crawl.

The elastrator looks like a pair of pliers, except that its head is a tightly gathered set of metal pins. A miniature rubber doughnut is slid over the pins. When handles are pressed together, the pins spread, opening the doughnut to a size that will slip over the tail. Or the whatever.

When I told Tom Deason I had this job to do in the sheep shed, he ambled along to help. Our plan was simple.

"I'll hold the lamb under my left arm, Tom, with the pliers in my right hand. You straighten the tail, and I'll slide on the pliers. Then you slide the band off the prongs, onto the tail."

"Right," said Tom, and we stepped into the shed.

Olive wasn't too happy when I picked up her lamb and swung it under my arm, nether end pointed toward Tom. She baa'd protests as Tom straightened the lamb's tail and I slipped the pliers down its length. Then Tom leaned in to ease the band off the circlet of pins. The band snapped neatly onto the tail.

It wasn't the lamb's fault, of course. I guess that sudden tightening on its tail just made other parts go slack. For an instant, though, I felt I was cradling a blunderbuss. And Tom, intent on his job, was right in the line of fire.

As I say, he's a man of good humor and shrugged the matter off—at least figuratively. But, next time he visits, I owe Tom a bottle of Canadian rye.

I figure a quart, at least.

27

A Woman of Determination

*M*urder drew me down to the Milford Central School recently. I'd heard about a talk to be given there that evening by writer Niles Eggleston, a respected authority on the Town of Milford history and folklore. Mr. Eggleston's engaging subject was Otsego County's own "Trial of the Century"—one that had Cooperstown and its environs on the country's front pages even before the National Baseball Hall of Fame and Museum.

Of course I'm talking about the case of Eva Coo, a lady whose name might suggest Eden and lovebirds, but who was a very cool and businesslike murderess. I'd heard a half dozen versions of her story since moving here, some of them contradictory. Now, at last, I was going to get the real skinny from Mr. Eggleston.

Niles has a book out on Eva Coo; you'd enjoy it. He is a very careful researcher and a grand story teller. That night he told us that Eva was born in Ontario, Canada, in 1893 and did nurse's training and married in Toronto. Neither nursing nor marriage suited her, it seems. Eva shrugged off both while living in Calgary, Alberta, and headed down here to develop her real talent: running bars and brothels.

Prohibition brought her great success with both vocations in Oneonta. Eva's patrons included a full range of the town's male populace—from well-known politicians and businessmen to college students and draymen. But a shift in political winds, said Niles, suddenly had policemen raiding her place instead of patronizing it. So in 1928 she moved operations a few miles into the countryside, opening the Woodbine Cafe about four miles north of Colliersville. Prohibition was at its height, and many were willing to take a little country drive for bootleg booze and for services offered in a line of cabins behind the Woodbine.

Then came 1933 and disaster. The Congress, in a rare lucid moment, ended Prohibition; the bottom fell out of bootlegging. Eva, then turning forty, was suddenly very short of cash. But, ever resourceful, she turned to murder.

Living at the Woodbine with Eva, her paramour, and three ladies of the trade was Harry Wright, the slow-witted sixty-year-old son of a friend of Eva's. Eva had promised the friend at her deathbed to look out for Harry. As it turned out, it was Harry who needed to look out. Eva quickly ran through the little money Harry had, including what came from insurance on his mother's home, which had suddenly burnt.

That bit of insurance money got Eva thinking of another way she might capitalize on Harry. After getting him to sign a will making her his sole inheritor, Eva took out a total of

twenty insurance policies on Harry, each naming either her or his estate as beneficiary. Then, with her three lady associates, she took poor Harry for a ride, literally, to a deserted farm on Crumhorn Mountain.

There she got Harry out of the auto and brained him from behind with a wooden mallet. Harry fell forward in front of the idling car. At Eva's calm direction, Martha Clift, whose only previous experience at rolling stiffs had been in taking their wallets, put the car into first gear and slowly drove over Harry, front and rear wheels. Then, at Eva's firm urging, she slowly backed the rear wheels over him again. Eva was thorough.

They dumped Harry alongside the highway, and troopers first thought it was a hit-and-run. But closer examination showed Harry hadn't been hit by anything (except on the head). He did seem to have been run over, though. Carefully. Repeatedly.

Well, said Niles, troopers searched Eva's digs and found the sheaf of policies. A trial in Cooperstown soon followed. Eva was found guilty of murder—during a press frenzy to rival O. J. Simpson's trial. Condemned to death, Eva Coo was shipped to Sing Sing the next day, and she was electrocuted within the same year.

Niles Eggleston wonders about the haste of Eva's removal from both Otsego County and earth. In her Cooperstown cell, she had threatened darkly to name her prominent Oneonta clients. No question of her guilt, of course. But was Eva sent to death to silence her? Martha Clift, after all, got a sentence of only fifteen years.

Anyway, I think Milford's missing a chance. If, twenty miles to the north, Cherry Valley can re-enact a colonial massacre, why can't Milford mint some coin from the Crumhorn murder? Think of profits from just the T-shirts—the ones with tire tracks across the back.

28

The Picking Ritual, Getting Outfoxed

*S*ome people are hinged differently from me. I learned that fact while down at Paul Ingall's Farm in Hartwick Seminary, gathering strawberries. In the second half of June, Paul's pick-'em-yourself fields are full of folks of every age. They start arriving in the early morning mists, park field-side in neat rows, and pony up a modest fee to fill four-quart baskets with ripe berries. Smiling young girls with walkie-talkies manage the fields, assigning each newcomer to a specific section of a row.

The picking ritual is simple but strict. You move down the row, picking berries on your right side and your left. You're not supposed to reach into any berry bush beyond its midpoint, since the other side belongs to the picker in the next row. I reached too deep once and the lady in the next row hit me with a five-hundred-watt glare. I didn't do that twice.

The talk that came drifting across the rows sounded near to ritual, too. I guess the same sentences are spoken in those rows every year:

"Berries this year are nice and big, aren't they." And "Looks like you're eatin' more than you're savin'." And, plaintively, "Momma, you said this was gonna be fun!"

Earlier I mentioned people's hinges. Strawberries grow at ground level; and pickers, I noticed, divided into squatters, benders, and crawlers. The squatters crouched low, like umpires, and duck-walked down their rows. When their knees began to cramp, they'd brace hands on them and slowly straighten up. Sometimes their poor knees cracked like rifle shots—you'd hear the report two or three rows away, accompanied by, "Oh Lord! I ought to stop doin' this every year." Then sympathetic laughter.

Some squatters, most of them women, I noticed, had awesome stamina. They'd hold a crouch ten or fifteen minutes. I wonder if they trained all winter for berrying, squatting through whole Oprah shows, duck-walking over to the set to change the channel.

The women were the best benders, too. Benders locked their knees, dropped straight over from the waist, and moved along, picking that way. I gave that a try but couldn't keep it up long without shin splints starting.

Two white-haired gents in rows near mine were surprisingly good benders, though they did alternate with some squatting. Their talk took my mind off stinging tendons.

"Friend of Bud Hurley's dropped dead doin' this."

"What, pickin' berries?"

"Naw, bendin'. Come out his front door and bent over to tie his shoe. Had a big vein blow out in his head. Neighbor found him on the porch, slumped down on his knees and his nose."

"Not a bad way to go."

"What, in a heap with your rump in the air?"

"Naw, fast. Hope I go that way."

"Well, don't do it now. I just wanna get done here and go get breakfast."

Two-thirds through my basket, I was ready to give up on squatting and bending and throw in my lot with the crawlers. These had shelved self-consciousness and dropped to all fours, resting their weight on their left hand to pick with the right, then reversing to pick the other side. They pushed the basket along the row ahead them and crept after it. Crawlers seemed to be the really serious, single-minded pickers. Not much talk out of them.

In fact, it was a crawler who had burned me with that high-voltage glare.

Finally done, I stood to a two-gun salute from my own knees. The same crawler lady smiled sideways up at me, all gracious now that I wasn't a potential poacher.

"Berries are beautiful this year, aren't they," she said.

I smiled back and nodded, looking down at my heaped basket. I knew the ritual answer.

"They really are—and worth the work."

◆ ◆ ◆

Domestic tragedy, first thing the other morning. I was snatched from sleep at six A.M. by wild shrieks and squawks from back by the barn. Terror! Panic! Despair!

I jumped up groggily, blundered down the stairs and into the yard. Halfway down the flagstone walk, I saw sudden, blurred movement ahead of me, down across the lawn near the barn. (My glasses, of course, were back upstairs, on the bedside table.)

Something bulky shaped, a mix of reddish-brown and yellow went rushing off across the stubble of the hayfield and into the woods. What was it?

I walked barefoot down the wet lawn. On the grass I found a four-foot circle of chicken feathers. At its center was a bit of blood.

Shaking my head sadly, I walked over to the chicken yard. Inside it was chaos—chickens milling and squawking at one another, no doubt recounting the awful thing they'd seen. I could make no sense of it, so I took roll instead. Rooster? Present. Five hens? Present, plus chirping chicks under one of them. Missing and unaccounted for was one handsome young cockerel.

Too bad. I'd had plans for him. They involved the chopping block and fricassee pot.

In a small flock, a second rooster is one too many, and this youngster was just about to come of age. I'd already seen him sparring with the senior bird, double his size and his weight. So I'd decided to solve a pair of problems: flock dynamics and what's-for-supper.

Not now, though. Something had reduced roosters to one—and someone was now having my supper for breakfast, down by the creek.

I saw how the luckless cockerel had got out of the yard: a break in the chicken wire. He'd found it and, cocky young bird, gone for a stroll in the morning dews and damps. Bad mistake, that.

As he was strutting around, probably preening for the hens watching through the fence, something had crept up and pounced. That ring of scattered feathers suggested he'd put up a short, tough struggle. But whatever grabbed him was tougher yet.

But what was it?

Of course I called in a detective. Midmorning, Arrie Hecox arrived on the crime scene. He studied it closely. Arrie's been warring with farm varmints for four-score years.

He scowled at the circle of feathers, questioned me closely. I felt as inept as those witnesses on "Law and Order," who always end by saying, with a helpless shrug, "It all happened so fast!"

I did tell Arrie about the reddish-brown and yellow blur, and about my glasses back upstairs. He smiled grimly and pointed at the feathers.

"The yellow part was that bird," he said brusquely. "The reddish-brown was the killer, hauling it off." He stood for a moment, thumbs hooked in bib overalls pockets.

"Which way did it run?" And again I pointed straight across the hayfield and into the woods. Another pause.

"Fox," he pronounced firmly. "A dog, when he saw you, would've run straight up or down the field to get away—and probably toward the road. But a fox would head straight for cover. You got a fox to worry about."

There. Fox behavior versus a dog's. Another useful country fact learned from Arrie. But a fox—that was a serious matter. Especially one that had feasted on a young bird and knew where there were more.

I fixed the broken spot in the chicken fence, walked the perimeter, strengthening spots where a fox might get in. And there'd have to be a chicken curfew now. No more leaving the coop door open at night, treating the birds to night breezes. They'd have to be shut in at dark, loosed at dawn.

Oh, well. The fox had spared me the mess of the block,

spared me plucking and drawing and chilling the bird. But, damn it! He'd had my dinner for me, too.

I'd planned parsley dumplings. And fresh green beans from the garden. And probably beets...

29

Despite the Odds, Here I Am

Sometimes, on the screened porch, feet propped up, sipping iced tea, I wonder at the chain of causes that brought me to be in Fly Creek—or, for that matter, simply brought me to be. For instance:

I had supper last month at Great-Grandpa's house down in tidewater Maryland. It's a handsome brick house with dormers, and it used to face a clear view across the fields to broad West River. But the area grew, and the fields filled up with houses for commuters to Washington. And Great-Grandpa's house is now a restaurant—a classy French one, mind you, down there in Shady Side, at one time home only to small farmers and men who fished, oystered, and crabbed on the Chesapeake Bay.

We ate in an expansive, open-beamed addition to the house, built out over the old backyard. It was tasteless of me, but I couldn't help saying, "You know, the privy would have stood right over there, between the hat rack and the waiter's station."

My fellow diners grimaced and went back to their goat's cheese and endive vinaigrette. But I still sat back, fascinated. "And this table," I added, "is probably placed just about over the old well."

If we were above that well, I was at a spot crucial to my life. For about 1880, a toddler, Great-Grandpa's youngest daughter, fell down the family well. My grandmother.

As little boys, my brother and I would sit open-mouthed as she told the story—which she only knew from adults who repeated it later, shaking their heads. She'd been playing in the sunny backyard with another little girl and perhaps meant only to look curiously down into the well's darkness. But she tumbled in, head first.

The other tot came into the busy kitchen, pulled at her own mother's dress. "Annie Owings is down the well," she lisped. The women ran shrieking into the yard. Neighbors' doors banged open and a half dozen people rushed to stand around the well hole, peering down in horror.

The little girl was almost completely submerged. Only one foot jutted above the water in a tiny, high-button shoe.

Men bent themselves over the well rim, stretching, clawing down toward the water. But the shoe was just out of reach, even for the tallest of them. Then a voice said, "Lemme try, cap'ns." And a tall black farmer stepped to the well, drawing from his pocket a button hook. He leaned over the well rim, bent his torso down into the darkness. He reached down with the hook, stretched himself even farther, snagged the shoe's topmost button. And drew Annie Owings back from death.

"They rolled me on a barrel to get the water out," Grandma would say, "and finally I coughed and sputtered, and then I started to cry."

I told Grandma's story to my table, and we sat silent. Then we toasted her, and that button hook. And the tall black man, name unknown, who saved her life. And who opened life to my father, my brother, and me.

I've thought of it often since that meal. An event sixty years before my birth almost meant I wasn't. No big loss for the world, I know—but a considerable one for me.

How many other near misses, I wonder, were there for me, back across all those countless generations? Beyond the ancestors who might have been snuffed by wars, plagues, and falls down wells, what were my chances that all the right conceptions would take place, across all those endless generations? It's dizzying, strikes me wordless.

And makes me wonder about a human's value. Maybe each of us should say, "What am I worth? I'm only here by sheer blind luck." Or maybe the opposite: "I must mean something since, despite unthinkable odds, here I am."

Here we are, between darknesses, gifted for awhile with life.

Maybe we owe something by that fact to all those faceless ghosts—those who could have been. But never were.

30

Head Over Heels Over Maggie

ast month I tried my hand at shearing a sheep. Probably it'll come out better next time. This time I had to call in a local pro to finish the job. John Craig, from Oaksville, is only just out of high school, heading for Lehigh University; but he's dealt with sheep for at least half his life. Experience counts in sheep-shearing.

John's a fine, polite young man—and tactful, too. Out of respect for my feelings, I'm sure, he started with the poor sheep I'd worked on. I'd left Maggie looking like a bad day at the barber college: bare skin here, lumpy tufts there, stringy strands sticking out or drooping down. For the first day after her haircut, even Maggie's own lambs hadn't been sure who she was; they'd kept their distance from her. I only hope she didn't catch her reflection in the water trough.

Young John cleaned up Maggie in no time. When he'd finished, she was as clean-shaven as a boot-camp recruit; but she looked like a respectable sheep again. Then John turned his attention to Maude and Mary and soon had them groomed like 4-H entries.

John handled the three sheep the classic way: rolled each on its back, set it up on its butt, got a hammerlock around its neck and one leg, and started on the underside. Clippers buzzed, fleece fell away before long strokes. As John worked, each sheep baa'd—but resignedly, I thought. They'd all been through shearing before. Perhaps they had dim memories of feeling better, cooler, afterward. I watched John's skill and tried not to think back on my own ham-handed work.

In that botched attempt, I'd had good help. My farming mentor Arrie Hecox was there; and Greg Byrer, an old friend from college days, had come over from Portland, Maine. Greg had something to laugh about on the long drive home.

We plugged the big clippers into a long lead cord, spread a tarp in a corner of the pasture, and drew the sheep over with a pan of grain. That's when I took leadership, and I grabbed Maggie by the scruff of the neck.

Maggie, a big sheep, didn't like being grabbed. She took off in a tight circle and got me airborne, my boots cutting a broad arc through the warm air. Then, clever old sheep, she stopped dead. I didn't. I cleared her back and landed hard, halfway onto the manure heap.

I asked Greg later what he was thinking as I sailed around Maggie's head. Greg makes his living with a counseling practice and is as tactful as young John. "I was wondering," he said quietly, "why you didn't let go."

While I was brushing off myself as best as I could, Greg

and Arrie got hold of Maggie and eased her over on her side. I fired up the clippers, knelt by the sheep, and started in.

It's all in the angle of the blades, I learned later, watching John. Decisive strokes, with blades tipped a bit toward the skin. But I was a novice, clipper-shy, afraid of cutting into skin instead of wool. I did my best, though conditions weren't ideal. I was aching from Maggie's judo throw. I smelled of lanolin and much worse. But grim and determined, I worked away against a background of plaintive baa's, encouraging words from Greg's end of the sheep, acerbic ones from Arrie's.

After a half hour, I didn't so much finish the job as abandon it. I straightened up painfully. Maggie struggled to her feet and stood there, looking horrific. Then she walked off stiffly, not once glancing back. Behind her, on the big blue tarp, there was nothing like a soft, full fleece—just lots of scattered knots and snarls of greasy wool. It looked like a sheep had exploded there.

Next summer I'll do better. I'll get a book, and read up on shearing. But on the other hand—if John Craig is home from Lehigh on vacation…

31

Old Man and Old Dog

A crowd filled Fly Creek church to remember a grand old man who'd died at eighty-nine. People leaving the service were amazed when they realized its length—almost two hours. During it, no one had thought of time. We'd been too gathered into recalling the departed: Barry Rumple, everyone's friend.

From pulpit and from pews, speakers praised Barry's warmth, quiet dignity, his unstudied gift for giving with heart and hands. As one of his sons said movingly, Barry's family was first beneficiary of his goodness; but so were neighbors, co-workers at NBC Television, even his sons' friends around their homes in New Jersey and then in Worcester, New York.

And so were Fly Creek and this area, when Barry and his late wife moved here in 1987. At eighty, he began finding new ways to serve, volunteering several days a week at Bassett Hospital, coordinating the local Meals on Wheels, sitting on non-profit boards. Three times in four years we saw him stunned by grief: by his wife's death, then his son's, then his grandson's. Each time, somehow, Barry shook his head clear and continued to give. And did so to within days of his death.

A grand example of Barry's goodness was read in the church—a letter, not from a Fly Creek neighbor, or even from New York State. The letter came from a Canadian family in Peterborough, Ontario, who grieved for their "U.S. Grandpa."

In 1984, Barry walked into his Worcester, New York, back-yard to find a limp helium balloon and, attached to it, a note from a Canadian boy.

"Will the finder of this balloon," ten-year-old Michael Keast had written hopefully, "please let me know where it landed?"

Barry did more. He wrote a long, enthusiastic letter to the little boy. And when Michael wrote back his thanks, Barry answered with another letter—and with the first of many small gifts crafted in his woodshop. There followed a wonderful pen-pal correspondence across twelve years, and even a visit by the Keast family to Fly Creek, and later by Barry, then a widower, to Peterborough.

When Michael went to University, his mother continued exchanging letters with Barry. She was answering his last, written days before his death, when the phone rang and she learned he was gone.

In his final year, failing health forced Barry to give up, one by one, his multiple community services. He was very unhappy about it.

"Jim," he said over coffee in his kitchen, "I've got to find something to do!" It wasn't a bored man complaining, but a man who lived to serve, and now hadn't strength for it.

He did continue his wide correspondence, even kept on balancing books for his old church back in Worcester. And he tried to take care of himself and his loyal sidekick: gentle, wise Goldie—as old in dog-years as Barry was in human.

From my desk by a second-floor window, I see a good way up Cemetery Road. Spotting Barry and Goldie, heaving into sight on their walks, was a daily event. Sometimes I'd flag them down for a visit. We'd sit in the back room, Barry listening, then responding in his slow, gravelly voice; Goldie sitting quietly beside his chair—and making an effort, so help me, to smile.

Most often, though, their walks went uninterrupted. They'd pass together below my window and head down Allison Road— to reappear, maybe twenty minutes later, heading slowly home.

As Barry's health weakened, the walks grew shorter. In the last months, the outward stretch ended in a U-turn below my window. And then the walks stopped.

That will be, I think, my abiding image of one of nature's noblemen: A blustery day, and the back of Barry in plaid wool jacket and cap. Earflaps down, shoulders hunched against the cold. Shuffling slowly away, up the road to home. Goldie, on a leash hardly needed, limping along ahead or, more often, right at his side.

Old man and old dog. Watching out for each other.

32

Still Backing
the Brave Lost Cause...

*Y*ou may wonder at it, but lately I've been thinking about joining the Army. The Farmers' Museum was advertising a living Civil War experience: twenty-four hours as a Union enlistee, including three meals of 1860's army cooking, plus drill and inspection, plus a chance to curl up and sleep, un-mattressed, in a period-style tent.

I was intrigued. Back in high school, I was a Civil War buff and collected swords, pistols, muskets, canteens, cap boxes—all much easier to come by in those days. And I still have a handsome Springfield muzzle-loader hanging over my mantle and a cavalry saber on the wall. Maybe I'd enjoy being a one-day soldier...

But wisdom prevailed; I decided I'm too old to enlist. After a night of tenting on the old campground, reveille might find me unable to stand, straighten up, and fall in. And, besides, if I joined the Union Army, even for a day, I'd be haunted by southern-ancestor ghosts, my grandmother in the lead.

As that tragic war began, my native state of Maryland almost seceded. But Mr. Lincoln foresaw an awkward condition: If Maryland went with the South, Washington would be surrounded by the Confederacy. And so Abe acted, if not legally, with great effect. He put Maryland's governor under house arrest; and he surrounded the nervous State Legislature, just about to vote, with a solid ring of grim-looking federal troops. Prudent men, the legislators voted to stick with the North.

But lots of southern Marylanders made their own choice, and many enlisted in Virginia regiments. This included kin of mine—though not one great-great uncle, a carpenter, who didn't sign on with Ol' Robby Lee and who also dodged the Union draft. (He bolstered the southern cause by hightailing it north to Philly for the duration—to build, no doubt, deliberately shoddy housing for the enemy.) Its understandable that Grandma didn't talk much about him.

But she had lots of stories about the war. Born eleven years after it, she'd grown up on her parents' tales of privations and Yankees' harassment of decent southern Marylanders. Great-Grandpa had kept a general store and post office; and in her old age his daughter would still clench her thin fists as she recounted stories of Yankee outrages on him—arrogant soldiers swaggering into the store to commandeer, mind you, all the flour, sugar, and butter.

"Why," she'd say, tight-faced, "they'd even just take things for spite—things they'd no use for, like big bolts of yard goods. Papa said that once, as they rode off, an insolent soldier sat on the wagon tailgate, grinning back at him and my Mama. Then that soldier reached back behind him and grabbed hold of a whole bolt of calico. He flung it back, off the wagon, but still holding onto the loose end. The bolt flapped in the air, unfolding, and then it fell in the road dust and manure. And that Yankee just threw back his head and laughed!"

Such memories were nursed down there, when people still grieved the brave Lost Cause. A broken hinge on the spring house door, proof of the oppressor's heel, was deliberately left unrepaired for decades.

So you see, even setting aside sleeping on the hard ground, I couldn't enlist in The Farmers' Museum brigade. I couldn't don the Union blue, even for the day.

Grandma's ghost would rank me with that shameful uncle who hid out in Philly. And maybe I'd never get another good night's rest, with mattress or without.

33

Shall a Hyphen
Come Between Us?

'*I*'ve been musing, on and off, about surnames—ever since Anne and I sat down with the Town Clerk to fill out our marriage license. Pam Deane typed facts and figures into her computer and, lo! our vital stats appeared on the screen in ghostly gray, filling blanks on the State's official form. Places of birth, parents' names, citizenship—it was all there, including Anne's name, pre- and post-nuptial.

Though she will be using just Atwell socially, for business Anne has decided she'll be Geddes-Atwell. Hanging onto the Geddes for her work makes good sense to me. Old customers are used to it. And since it is a classic Scottish name, it has a no-nonsense, cost-conscious tone. Clients must like that.

Further, there's another Anne Geddes abroad in the design world: a New Zealand woman who's made boxcars of money with a line of photo-greeting cards. You've seen them: small babies, almost smothered in frills, gazing uncertainly out of overturned baskets, pumpkins, bird nests, and the like.

To me, the cards seem creepy, even vaguely perverse—and sugary enough to bring on diabetes. But, as I say, the New Zealand Anne Geddes is minting money with them around the globe—and who knows? Perhaps one of those royalty checks could get misdirected and pass through the Fly Creek Post Office. That's another good reason for my Anne to hang onto her own name...

Anyway, my musings about surnames recalled a fine wry story, from some twenty years in my past. Let me share it, after a brief pedantic flourish.

Surnames, we're told, aren't that old an invention; they came about to set off this John or Janet from a dozen others of the same name. Often they identified someone by trade (whence all the Bakers, Smiths, Thatchers, Hunters, Sawyers, and Cooks in any large phone book.) And sometimes they were topographical (like my own prosaic last name, kin to Atwater, Bywater, Stillwell, etc.).

But a secondary use of surnames quickly developed: to identify, not just individuals, but families. Maybe John Baker's great-grandson didn't make bread, but his surname still linked him to the family clan—and its inheritance line. That promoted stability and continuity—useful features in an ordered society.

About thirty years ago, when we lurched into a kind of national bad trip, stodgy old concepts like "stability" and "continuity" were shrugged off by the carefree hippies and their imitators. In that loopy aquarian age, individual rights were enthroned, and common-good values eclipsed. We are, I think, still getting over all that.

Sometime in the early nineteen-eighties, I ran into a relic of Woodstockism. It was still alive and oddly embodied in a hippie turned yuppie—turned, in fact, into an edgy, successful streetfighter of a lawyer. She was steering a group suing our college. One morning, before the day's depositions got under way, she gave her shark's smile and told us about a minor family crisis.

When she was pregnant with their first child, she and her husband had vowed they wouldn't inflict either of their surnames on a new, unique human—as if it were their possession. Instead, with what they judged great wisdom, they took a syllable from each of their surnames and created a third, new surname: Randsill. And, in fullness of time, their offspring was named Jonas Randsill.

Now, said the lawyer, some five years later, she had become pregnant with her second child. Little Jonas had come to his mother and asked what the child's name would be. "Well," said his mother, "if it's a little boy it will be Richard, if a little girl, Rebecca."

"No," said Jonas, scowling. "What will its last name be?"

"Why, Randsill," said Mom. The little boy went red-faced, beat the table with his fists. "No it won't!" he screamed. "That's my name!"

Don't you love it when people's smugness comes full circle and bites them in the butt?

Well, that story is about surnames, but there's no other link to Anne's choosing to hang onto Geddes. In fact, I really like her name nudged up close against mine.

And the hyphen? Why, no scrawny punctuation mark could ever divide us.

34

What was Meant to Be?

I think I have just seen Darwinian selection at work. Or maybe "Nature's way." Whatever its proper name, the experience has left me awed.

This time last year, brand new to sheep, I was waiting for my three ewes to deliver. I'd pored over *Raising Sheep the Modern Way.* I'd assembled a kit with everything the author said I might need for births. I'd memorized the list of awful things that could go wrong, and what to do in each case. I was prepared.

For nothing. In fact, all three ewes delivered in the middle of the night, and each following morning I came out to the sheep shed to find tottering new lambs nursing contentedly, mothers looking relieved and proud.

This year, Maude, my elderly horned Dorset, was the first due, and I guess I expected to have an easy time again. Not so. Maude went into labor mid-morning and was quickly in bad trouble—beyond anything I could help with. I phoned Dr. Fassett, and shortly the vet pulled into my yard with his son Derek.

While Derek and I held Maude, the vet checked her and said the first of twin lambs was reversed and the two were tangled in the womb; both would have died within the hour. As it was, he got the lamb turned and delivered the twins—only to spot a further problem: Maude had no milk to give them.

Milk substitute was as close as the Agway farm supply store. The real problem was lack of what lambs should get with their first mother's milk: colostrum, a rich mixture of nutrients and antibodies almost essential for survival. At Dr. Fassett's suggestion, I headed up Christian Hill to Jim and Eileen McCormack's sheep farm.

Eileen had no frozen colostrum on hand and no luck phoning around for some. I rushed home to start the lambs on the sheep book's emergency substitute—evaporated milk, water, sugar, castor oil, and egg yolk. I'd hardly begun feeding them when Eileen arrived, carrying a baby bottle of milk she'd got from one of her ewes. Better than nothing, she said.

We sat and watched Maude, who, whenever approached by one of her lambs, lay down, blocking access to her empty udder. Eileen, who's been midwife to sheep by the hundreds, shook her head.

"You know," she said, "maybe these lambs weren't meant to live. Maude knows she's got nothing to give them."

Well, I set myself to bottle-feeding the lambs with milk substitute, every two hours, day and night. Every time I entered the shed, I'd find Maude motionless, legs folded under her. Her gaze was fixed. She ignored the lambs. At four o'clock the second morning, I came in to find the smaller lamb, a male, lying still and already stiff. Despite my efforts, it hadn't been in him to live.

I thought the second would make it, but she must have aspirated some milk into her lungs. Two o'clock the third morning found her stumbly and wheezing. By 10 A.M. she was mewling feebly and suffering badly. I put her down.

I took that second little body from the shed and came back to find Maude standing, looking around. When I lowered the gate on the birthing pen, she walked out, paused, then went out the shed door into the sunshine. And began eating for the first time since she'd given birth.

They were not meant to live, Eileen had guessed; and Maude, from the start, had agreed. No, I don't mean she made a conscious decision. But from the time that terrible labor began, something in Maude knew that, if they lived, the lambs would be weak—and she had no way to strengthen them. And so she lay down. And waited. And when it was over, Maude went back to the flock.

By coincidence, Maggie began labor early that afternoon. She delivered a big male, and I put both of them in the birthing pen. After an errand to the house, I came back to find she'd delivered a ewe as well. Maggie was licking them clean, humming to them from deep in her throat, as new mother sheep do. Soon both lambs had heads under her, punching contentedly at her bag.

While I watched, Maude came into the shed. She stood looking into the pen, as if newborn lambs were something she'd never seen before. Then she turned and went back into the sunshine.

◆ ◆ ◆

Two days later, another lamb arrived—and I delivered it. It was Mary's lamb, but there was nothing "little" about it. Mary herself is a dainty cheviot, with billowy fleece ending above her knees and just behind her ears. Her dark eyes gaze from a face clean-lined, elegant, and covered, not with wool, but soft white hair.

She went into labor the day after Maggie had her twins, and, faithful to the sheep book, I sat and watched for a full hour as she struggled on her own. It just wouldn't work. By the time the big lamb's muzzle and front hooves had appeared, Mary was very near exhaustion and had almost stopped trying to push. Time now, the book said, to help.

I disinfected my hands and knelt next to her, taking the small hooves in one hand and slowly pressing back the muzzle. Now the lamb's legs—incredibly long!—could straighten. Mary obviously felt the change and began her work again. At each push, I pulled gently on legs and then head. And all at once, shoulders were free and out slid a beautiful ewe.

We mammals make a messy entrance into the world—blood, mucous fluids, membranous sac. But no matter. It was a fine, fine moment.

Mary thought so, too. As Maggie had the day before, she began at once to sing to her offspring, lovely soft rumbles from the back of her throat. After she'd cleared the lamb's mouth, it began to bleat in response to her song. I sank back into a folding chair and sat entranced. In minutes, the lamb had tottered to its feet and begun to nurse.

I know—to any 4H kids, this birthing business is routine stuff. But, hey, cut me some slack. I was fifty-eight and brand new to all this. I'd delivered a lamb!

But there's sad news, too. I told you that old Maude seemed to come to herself after losing her two lambs. And so she did, for a day. But then a decline set in. Again she stopped eating. For hours she'd simply stand in the sunny yard, head down, as the bustle of chickens and geese, ewes and lambs, eddied around her. She'd seemed to decide her lambs weren't meant to live. Now, perhaps, she'd decided her own time had come.

I thought about calling the vet. But no, Maude wasn't a pet. She was a farm animal, an old one, who certainly could not be bred again. And so I left her alone. Those who know animals only as pets may dissent. Farmers will slowly nod their heads.

It ended after a week. I found Maude lifeless, stretched on her side. While the other sheep stood watching, I crouched. I scratched her nose and told her she'd been a good sheep, the only eulogy I could think of. Then I tied together a rope's ends. I looped the rope under her horns, and then around my own shoulder.

Maude had lain a long way from the gate, and dragging the weight was work. The first time I stopped for breath, I looked back. Behind the body were the other three ewes, lined up, single file. When I began again to pull, they followed behind.

With two more pauses for breath, I led the procession to the gate, pulled Maude through, and closed it. The others bunched on the inside, ewes gazing out over the middle bar, three pink-nosed lambs over the bottom one.

I don't project human feelings into animals. So I don't mean to say that the file of sheep was a cortege. It just felt that way. To me.

35

Something Left Unsaid

A gray fall day, rain falling steadily. Back from a good visit down in Annapolis with my fiancée Anne, I'm upstairs in the barn, admiring the hundred and ten bales of stored hay that will feed the ewes across the snowy months. The hay's soft summer smell, the dim light and shadowed corners, the muffled drum of rain above make the big room feel cozy, sheltered.

The barn's upstairs has always been a special place to me, with its southern view of the back field and grazing deer, and a view east across the valley bottom and up the hills. It's a space full of memories of my life with my late first wife Gwen. When we bought Stone Mill Acres in the mid-'70s, we planned eventual retirement in Fly Creek. There was no imagining my moving here alone, a widower, to begin a different life.

From the start, we rented the house out to pay the mortgage and taxes. But we kept the barn's second floor for our own use and camped there when we came up from Annapolis.

The barn was wired and had water, and it was fairly easy to knock together a closet and a kitchen counter, and to install an old cast-iron sink. We furnished it with bed, a table, a few chairs. We added a hot plate and a camp toilet, and even a shower. The last was a black five-gallon water bag I'd put outside in the sun. Then I'd haul it upstairs and hang its nozzle out the hay mow door. We did our showering downstairs, standing in the blessed open air, watched over by all the trees on Christian Hill.

The best part of camping in the barn was bedding down under those shadowed rafters, going to sleep to the sounds of crickets, of dogs barking far up the valley, of the distant, melancholy bellow of a cow across Oaks Creek.

But we weren't alone sleeping in the barn. Mice, who'd made it home long before we did, hadn't moved out. But that was all right. Gwen was a country girl, unshaken by mice if they kept a respectful distance.

One chill night, though, I came awake lying on my back. Gwen was on her side, back to me, sound asleep. The moon was full, and I admired the rafters in the pearly light, then looked down the bed's length toward the glowing window. On a mound in the blankets made by my toes, silhouetted against the bright glass panes, was a mouse. It was sitting very still, facing the window—perhaps enjoying the moonlight like me.

I was delighted and tried to stay very still as well, but in the end I must have twitched a toe. The mouse started, leaped backward away from the toe—and ran up the length of me, only to collide with my beard. It gave a terrified squeak and leaped sideways, right onto Gwen's shoulder. Then it ran down the length of her and leaped off the bottom of the bed. Gwen barely stirred in her deep sleep.

"Dear Lord," I thought, "if she knew what just happened, she'd never spend another night here..."

The next morning Gwen nudged me gently awake.

"Shhh," she said. "Look over there on the stair railing." I eased up slowly in the bed and saw a mouse—I presume, the mouse—sitting on the rail. It was facing us, staring. From across the room, I couldn't see its expression, but there was something reproachful about the set of its shoulders.

"They're really cute, aren't they," Gwen whispered. "I guess that's as close to us as he dares to come."

"Guess so." I said. And no more.

Well, the furniture's piled in one corner up here now; fragrant hay bales fill up half the space. And my Gwen's gone almost eight years. But I can picture the hay vanished, the furniture back in place. And recall the fun we two had here— on many visits after the night of the mouse.

For I never told her about it. I hope that was all right.

36

All the Way Back to Adam

I have a Father's Day story for you, sent to me by a treasured friend who lives in California. He's a generous-hearted man and won't mind my sharing it with you, I know.

Dick taught me college English a long time ago. That was at La Salle, down in Philadelphia. Four decades later, he's just retired from a West Coast college. Back then, Dick was in his twenties, maybe six years older than his students, a young father with a growing family. Now Dick and Fran's big brood, long grown, has the next generation well under way; and they're enjoying grandparenthood.

We've corresponded across all those years; I guess Dick has never stopped teaching me about writing. His letters are always encouraging—and, of course, models of how words ought to be used. In a recent one he talked about one of his sons, who'd had a somewhat troubled youth. Dick and Fran had done their best, worried and prayed about their boy, and finally just entrusted him to Providence.

The boy's married now, a new father, and the miracle's happened. He wrote to Dick, telling him fatherhood had opened his eyes to all Dick had been to him. The young man wrote page after page (with something of his father's gift), outlining how his life had been redefined by having a son.

Dick sent me his son's letter and his own moving reply, full of warmth and congratulation and humor, too. Its high point (and what I want to share with you) was Dick's recounting his first child's birth, which he just missed witnessing.

He was to have been there, holding Fran's hand in the

delivery room; but she was rushed to the hospital while Dick was at work. In near panic, Dick ran out of his building and flagged a cab. He rode the few miles in desperation, wrenched this way, then that, by joy and anxiety, excitement and dread that he wouldn't get there in time. Bursting into the maternity ward, he ran right into the smiling black nurse who'd instructed Fran and him for this day.

"Hold it, honey!" she said firmly, grabbing his shoulders. "You can't just go in there in street clothes! You'll contaminate the whole place." She thrust a white hospital gown at him and pushed him into a room. "You just get that gown on," she sternly commanded.

Dick did. In mindless panic, he stripped himself bare, plunged arms into the gown sleeves, ran flapping through the door and down the hall. The nurse let out a whoop of glee.

"Hold on, Poppa! I meant put it over your clothes! You're not having the baby!" She tied the gown's back and steered him to the delivery room door. Too late. Dick pushed it open to hear his first son's first cry.

What a wonderful letter that was! Dick addressed his boy as a peer, as another father. Now an aging man, he spoke with wonder of his own life—"as son, man, husband, father, advanced into years hardly dreamed of in my youth." The letter celebrated the blessed continuity of life, and celebrated men's place in it. It made me sit a long time and think of James Agee's *A Death in the Family* (first read as Dick's student forty years before).

Early in that book, a father has come into his little boy's room to soothe away the sobs a nightmare caused. He sits on the bedside, cradling his son, and sings him back to peaceful sleep. And as he sings to the boy, he reflects that, just so, his dad had sung to him, and his dad's dad before him—as dads have sung to sons, he thought, all the way back to Adam. Who, sadly, had no dad to sing to him.

Except, perhaps, God did.

37

A Marriage Well Begun

Two mornings after Anne's and my perfect wedding, I woke up with a rotten head cold—clogged nose, sore throat, the works. How's that for knocking the edge off romance? So far Anne hasn't caught it from me. But imagine the ways it has compromised our togetherness! (On second thought, don't.)

Never mind, the wedding was wonderful. It was abridged to essentials: couple, minister, two witnesses. We wanted an intimate ceremony, so we'd told our friends we were eloping. And elope we did.

But not far. Only to the hayfield beyond the barn and sheep shed. I'd mowed a bridal path to a high spot in the field, and cut a twelve-foot circle there. We edged its south side with an arc of potted mums; and Anne and I stood there on a sunny autumn afternoon, facing the Reverend John Blackman of Edmeston. Beyond him spread the waving grass, edged by reddening sumac and dark woods, and domed by a cloudless blue sky.

Rev. John and I had gone first to the site, to await the two-person procession from the house. With us was best man Arrie Hecox, buttoned tight in a dark wool suit and wearing his all-purpose scowl. Arrie and John waited in the mowed circle. I stationed myself where path met back lawn, watching for the procession.

And there it came: First, Anne's cousin Joan, carrying a small bouquet. Joan couldn't abide a wedding procession without music. And so, in a soft, lovely soprano, she sang a Scottish

air as she walked slowly down the green lawn, under the butternut and the larch, past the red barn and the yard of curious chickens.

Behind her came Anne, who stopped my breath with an outfit I hadn't been allowed to see: a fitted silk jacket of aubergine (as I was later told); more aubergine and ocher in her silk paisley skirt—even an aubergine ribbon trimming a golden straw hat. She was carrying a bouquet bright with golds and wheats and whites, and accented with sprigs of Scottish heather. She was smiling radiantly.

I'm glad Joan was doing the singing. It would have been beyond me. I could barely breathe.

Anne took my arm. We walked down the path to the circle and stood before John, my good friend for twenty-five years. Joan read Psalm 104, celebrating all of creation as we stood in its bright midst. And Arrie Hecox, tough, crusty, and deeply devout, read the Beatitudes with an eloquence that made my eyes brim. Vows were spoken, rings exchanged. And contrary to his threat, Arrie didn't deliberately drop Anne's ring in the grass so I'd have to hunt on hands and knees. ("Then you'd remember your wedding," he'd said.)

John pronounced us married, and it was done. Back to the house we went, for tea, coffee, and a Canadian wedding tradition: rich fruitcake with marzipan icing. (You'll remember that my bride was born in Calgary, Alberta.)

Supper that evening was by candlelight at Cooperstown's Otesaga Hotel. Newlyweds and witnesses were joined by Peg Famulare and Maxine Potts, both of them close Fly Creek friends. We sat in the vast dining room, before the handsome fireplace. Arrie Hecox's opening blessing carried enough spiritual wattage to sanctify the whole hotel. There were toasts and good wishes. Our friends talked and laughed through a delicious meal, and Anne and I sat in wonder that what we'd been waiting for had finally happened.

Then our friends went home to their beds, and we to ours. And two mornings after, I woke to that rotten cold. What a way to start a marriage!

"Not to worry," said my bride. "You and I vowed 'for better or worse.' We are just getting 'worse' out of the way, first thing."

As I've said, she's my kind of woman.

❖ ❖ ❖

The idea—the inspiration—came from somewhere in the Fly Creek Area Historical Society: Let's resurrect a grand old custom, and let's celebrate with it!

Anne and I, one week married, were settled on the sofa late one evening, watching an "X-Files" rerun. Suddenly, from out front, came a blast of car horns. I jumped up. An accident, I thought. Someone must have run the Cemetery Road stop sign—must have swung in front of a car speeding uphill from Oaks Creek bridge.

But outside the front window I saw headlights of, not two

cars, but three—no, four—no, more! In a beeline, they bar-reled right up our drive.

The driveway horseshoes around the house, and by the time Anne and I got to the backporch, we were surrounded with honking cars and people tumbling out—laughing, ring-ing bells, blowing bugles and whistles, banging tin cans and sauce pans. Friends, neighbors, all grinning, laughing.

"You know what this is?" a voice shouted. "It's a shivaree!"

The word is in your Webster's: "a mock serenade with ket-tles, pans, horns, and other noisemakers given for a newly married couple." And the custom is as old, I guess, as human history: Celebrate with the bride and groom—but salt it with good-humored harassment, too. The Greeks did it, and the Romans. In medieval times a rowdy crowd swept new bride and groom from wedding feast to bedroom door—and partied outside it all night, while the newlyweds, presumably, tried to focus attention elsewhere.

The American country version, still practiced some around here, is often called "belling" or "horning," as our avalanche of guests later explained. For after the tumult died down, they'd all crowded into our house to load the din-ing room table with snacks and sweets. A party, a wonderful, wholly unexpected party was under way.

The old way for horning, they said, was for the celebrators to sneak up on the newlyweds' house around one A.M. on wed-ding night or just after return from a honeymoon. The silent crowd surrounded the house, and some, ideally, climbed qui-etly on top of porches and roof. Then, at a signal, they started the raucous concert.

"You let 'em know you were happy for them," said one older friend "—and knew just what they were doin' in there!"

"I hope we made enough noise tonight!" shouted another, and added, "We won't worry about anybody calling the law on us—we got both Town Justices right here!" And there they were: a beaming Jim Wolff, loading appropriate music into our C.D., and good old Pat Yourno, recounting adventures at past shivarees.

The talk and laughter went on for an hour and a half; then friends were hugging, wishing us well, saying good-bye. They pulled out with a last fanfare of car horns, and Anne and I sank back in living room chairs, delighted, dumbstruck. A week before, we'd been married by a minister in a quiet, private ceremony. But now, with amazing style, our Fly Creek friends had added their blessing.

What a good place to live!

I guess that evening was special fun for us since traditionally the shivaree is aimed at young newlyweds, prone to confusion and blushes. This time its subjects were not, one might say, unduly young. But never mind: the shivaree's more earthy aspect hadn't been neglected, as we found out when we finally climbed the stairs.

During the confusion, someone had slipped up there and short-sheeted our bed.

38

To Connecticut and Back

I've been to a wedding in Connecticut and come back to Fly Creek with two stories to tell you. Anne was unable to go along, and so I'll tell her, too.

The drive down was rainy: through the Catskills on Route 145, then seventy miles on big interstates, then forty more on Route 25, south to Fairfield. Wipers on, the whole way.

But the next morning weather cleared. After the service, we all followed the young couple out of the church into brilliant summer sunshine and then convoyed under blue skies to a country club with deep porches and panoramic views of green, rolling hills.

The bride is Italian, so food and drink were abounding, irresistible. Brian the groom (yesterday, it seemed, I watched him baptized!) and Jennifer the bride had a wonderful time at their wedding, making all the rest of us especially happy watching them. I ate too much, danced too much, raised too many toasts. The next morning, dull-eyed but very content, I headed back toward Fly Creek.

But not the same way. It wasn't a day for interstates, so I picked up Route 7, straight north through Connecticut and into Massachusetts. Up there, I thought, I would snag good old Route 20 and head west and home.

After thirty miles, Route 7 broke out of suburban traffic and tunneled under arching trees, following creeks and valley bottoms. I glided alongside the Housatonic for miles, and drove through lovely Berkshire towns. And later, sure enough, there was Route 20, spooling off toward the Hudson.

Then came my trip's second adventure. Forty miles east of Albany, New York was a place brand new to me: Hancock Shaker Village, Pittsfield, Massachusetts. It was home for 170 years to members of the United Society of Believers in Christ's Second Appearing.

The Shakers are gone now (only a half dozen remain in the world, in a village near Bethel, Maine), but Hancock Village is beautifully maintained by volunteers and a museum trust. Buildings and grounds are kept neat and spotlessly clean. ("No dirt in heaven," said the Shaker foundress, Mother Ann Lee.) In the many workshops, tools are arranged neatly on benches and walls as if waiting the Shakers' own second appearing.

As their formal name suggests, these celibate men and women were millenarians, who held themselves apart from the world's corruption and, on a daily basis, expected the world's end. That lifestyle's an old one, extending at least back to the Essenes before Christ, continuing through monasteries, nourished even today in some branches of Christian fundamentalism. Though started in England, the Shaker version grew and flourished in America, with nineteen villages like Hancock by the 1830s. Now it's almost all gone. Of thousands of committed members, only that serene handful up in Bethel, Maine.

I visited the barnyards and gardens, walked through the silent buildings. Then I sat alone in the meeting house, trying to imagine the community at worship there. It's a graceful, bright room, only about thirty by sixty feet. Men and women filed into it through separate doors. The hundred and fifty sat on backless benches and settled into profound quiet, awaiting the Spirit's touch. Then someone would feel that touch and rise to sing. And dance.

Benches would be pushed back, and straight ranks of Shaker men would dance toward the room's center in a strict, stylized pattern—hop, shuffle, step—as the women danced the same way toward them. And then the rows receded like waves, dancing backwards toward the walls, only to sweep solemnly forward again. It sometimes went on for hours, and they sang as they danced. The Shaker hymn that we know best is, of course, "'Tis a Gift to be Simple."

I sat for a long time in the silent room, gazing at barred oblongs of sunlight on the wide floorboards, trying to hear the singing, the thump and scuffle of three hundred feet. All that single-minded devotion—focused, not only in worship, but in every daily action. ("Hands to work, hearts to God," said Mother Ann.) Perfectionism, expressed in every cow milked, every meal cooked, every cabinet made.

Some years ago Hal Holbrook, about to open in the latest revival of *Our Town,* was interviewed on TV. Why, he was asked, do people still flock to a play about daily life of long-dead villagers in a tiny New England hamlet?

Holbrook smiled gently and said, "Those folk knew who

they were, where they were. They knew what they were for, where they were going." He shook his head. "And we all still hunger for all that, don't we?"

Driving away from the Shakers' home, I said Amen.

♦ ♦ ♦

I'm a Motel Eight kind of guy, but the night before the Connecticut wedding I had to stay in a really posh motor inn: room as large as Anne's and my downstairs, big sauna, big weight room, big indoor pool—and, of course, big bill. Anyway, after I'd settled in my room, I headed down to the restaurant for supper.

It was as ritzy as the rest of the place: subdued lighting, Vivaldi on the Muzak, heavy linen cloths and napkins, menus in padded leather covers.

At the next table, brightening the place considerably, was a quartet of gray-haired women, sipping wine and waiting to order. They were talking about local events, and so I told them I was there for a wedding and asked if they could give me directions to the church.

"Which one?" asked the closest. When I told her St. Leo's, she beamed.

"Hey, 'at's my parish! No sweat! I'll draw yuz a map." And she did, on a slip of notepaper headed "From the desk of HELEN." Soon I had all their names.

We're here for our last supper!" said Lena, from beyond Helen; and all four cackled. "See, we went to school together and—yuz won't believe this—we all just turned seventy." More cackling.

"So tomorrow our kids are sending us all on a trip—flying us to Seattle, and then we go on a boat ride, up along Alaska. Gonna see whales and glaciers and everything."

"Me, I don't trust these kids," said Rose, across from Lena. "I think they hatched this Alaska trip to get rid of us." She tried to scowl darkly. "You know, one of them Eskimo things—send the old fogies out on the ice and then leave 'em there to freeze."

"Tell you what!" said Agnes, leaning in front of Rose. She shook a finger. "If somebody says, 'I'll row yuz all ashore to see the glaciers,' I say, 'Forget it!'" They clinked their wine glasses in agreement.

Just then, a small movement just beyond Rose caught my eye. Something with a lot of legs was crawling down the ornate faux marble column next to her—descending in short darts, down toward the table's surface. It seemed notably out of place, what with the candlelight, very deep carpets, and high prices.

"Excuse me, Rose," I said, "but is that a bug on the column next to you?" She glanced, then swung back with a grin of malicious delight.

"'At's no bug!" she said. "'At's a cockroach!"

Rose was still grinning, but now she had blood in her eye. She had been battling cockroaches all her life, I'd guess. The others at the table must have been veterans of the same war because they all leaned back while Rose grabbed a leather-covered menu in both hands.

Wham! She slammed it against the column. The gunshot report turned heads all around the restaurant and brought a young waitress running, smiling worriedly.

"Is something wrong?" she asked.

"Not with us," Rose said blandly. "But this guy might need some help." She held up the leather folder toward the waitress. The cockroach, I guess, was covering a good deal of the

160

back. The young woman squeaked and cringed.

"Don't worry, honey," said Lena soothingly. "He ain't gonna hurt nobody. He got his own problems."

The waitress, biting her lip, took the menu with fingertips and tottered away, holding the folder well in front of her, bug-side down.

"Imagine!" said Rose. "Havin' to kill a cockroach in a fancy place like this. You wouldn't think they'd let them in!"

Helen put down her glass. "He musta made the reservation in some other bug's name." Still more cackling laugher, loud enough to turn all the heads again.

They finished dessert ahead of me, pushed back chairs, and gathered up purses to leave.

"Hey!" said Agnes, "we're goin' in the piano bar now—get some of those funny blue drinks." She grinned. "Why not? The kids are payin'!"

"Come on in when you're done," urged Lena, and I said I probably would join them.

But as I left the dining room, they were coming out the bar door, heading down the lobby arm-in-arm.

"Damned place is dead as a graveyard!" Rose shouted over her shoulder. "See ya! Enjoy that wedding!"

"Bon voyage!" I called after them. They crowded into the entryway, Agnes saying,

"Hey! How 'bout I row yuz all ashore to see the glaciers?" The answer drifted back in chorus.

"Forget it!"

39

Thanks, Anna and Sam...

*M*aybe Grandparents' Day is just the card marketers' way of making sales in slack September. But, whatever the day's origin, I want to honor my Grandparents Atwell and tell you about a quiet conspiracy between them.

You remember little Annie Owings, who fell down a well a good many pages back? Well, in 1894, Anna Owings was sent from her small tidewater Maryland hamlet to a finishing school in Cornwall-on-Hudson, New York. She was seventeen. Her father, the hamlet's grocer and postmaster, hoped the northern schooling would lead to a good marriage, one that would distance the family still more from the local crabbers, craftsmen, and farmers.

Instead, it led to Anna's falling in love with a college boy, to their brief engagement, to her being sent home abruptly from the boarding school. (Aunt Nellie, an old dragon who lived in Cornwall-on-Hudson, discovered the engagement and blew the whistle on it.) Anna, my grandmother, was heartbroken. Great-grandfather was enraged. And the other Shady Siders were delighted; their overreaching grocer had got just what he deserved.

After her thwarted romance, poor Anna lived quietly at home for seven years. Then she was given in marriage to Sam Atwell, a short, loud, bandy-legged carpenter. Her father must have ground his teeth, but Anna was already twenty-five. Time was running out for marriage of any sort.

I think they did come to love one another, though they were polar opposites. Sam was a truly good man but rough-cut, a

chewer of tobacco on construction sites and a smoker at home of harsh cigars. He was zestfully, imaginatively profane, and when I think of visiting them, I can hear Grandma's pained voice: "Sam, please don't swear in front of the boy!"

For though her finishing school time had been cut short, Anna still aspired to refinement in every way—in speech, in deportment, dress, and certainly, according to her lights, in home decoration. I remember their living room as curtained and dim, filled with brass knickknacks, furnished with sofa and chairs so overstuffed they looked drowned and bloated. They were covered in maroon plush, prickly to the legs of a small boy in short pants.

Grandpa Sam had his own easy chair in a corner, next to a huge Stromberg-Carlson cabinet radio. When I ran from our house to theirs in the evenings, I'd always find Grandpa settled there, puffing clouds of acrid smoke out into the room, listening to John Charles Thomas singing "The Lost Chord" or "Danny Boy."

Grandma would be in a chair across the room, at the far edge of the cloud, trying to enjoy the music and ignore the

163

smoke. I'd kiss her and then run to climb into Sam's lap, snuggling low to keep out of the way of his arm as it pivoted the cigar from mouth to brass ashtray and back again.

At some point during those visits Grandma would always get up and go out of the kitchen, perhaps just to get some fresh air. When she'd left, I'd wordlessly raise my hand, index and forefinger parted, and Sam would place the smoldering cigar between them. I'd put the soggy end in my mouth and sit, puffing wickedly, flicking ashes into the tray, trying to blow the perfect smoke rings Grandpa did.

Then we'd hear Grandma Anna coming back. Sam would whisper "Quick, boy!" and I'd slip the cigar back into his blunt, callused fingers. When Grandma quietly took her seat again,

we were as when she had left, I hunkered down in Sam's lap, he puffing away, relishing the "best G__ d__ baritone on God's green earth."

"Sam," she'd say wearily, "not in front of the boy."

She never knew about my smoking that cigar.

I thought that for years, until Grandpa was long dead and Anna in her late eighties. Then, a grown man, I was sitting one evening with her in the living room. Over the decades, the cigar smell had finally faded. At her side on that plush couch, I confessed.

"Grandma, remember when I used to sit on Grandpa's lap and we'd listen to John Charles Thomas?" She smiled and nodded in reminiscence.

"Well, back then, when you'd go out of the room for something, Grandpa used to let me puff on his cigar. It wasn't a trick on you—just something he and I shared. I loved doing it."

She placed a veined hand on top of mine. The wedding ring Sam gave her hung loose on her thin finger.

"Why," she asked, "do you think I went out of the room?"

40

"The Animals are Coming..."

Sometimes our senses trigger unexpected memories. The timbre of an overheard voice recalls a friend not seen for years. A whiff of perfume downshifts you into deep reminiscence. A song on the car radio evokes your whole junior prom: stiff shirt collar, crepe paper streamers, gardenia corsage, pink punch—the works.

Of course the grand literary is example is Marcel Proust. Biting into a rich cake, a madeleine, he's suddenly awash with childhood memories. I guess he hadn't had many madeleines since then, and the cake's special blend of texture and taste made synapses snap all through his brain.

You'll want to know that I'm subject to Proustian moments, too. I had one recently with animal crackers.

At dinner at my brother's house in Annapolis, my sister-in-law Shirley honored Anne's transfer to country life with a box of animal crackers at each place. "Barnum's Animals," mind you—small red-and-yellow box with a wagon of caged animals printed on each side. Grinning clown on top. ("For your own circus, cut out figures, fold on dotted lines.") A cotton cord handle, a useful grip for small hands.

My epiphany didn't hit me at dinner but on our way home to Fly Creek, smack in the middle of the Poconos. Anne was driving. I opened the small box, parted the waxed paper. I peered in at the tan shapes, all about the size of Scrabble tiles. I took out a rhino, its skin folds etched deeply into the dough. I bit its head off.

Well, I was not drowned in bittersweet memories, and I was

not reduced to quacking sobs. (As a Proustian, I'm pretty low-voltage.) But I recalled, in an instant, how much those cookies had once meant to me. As a reward for behaving in the grocery store. As a contact with the world of wild animals. And as something that tapped my infant drive for ownership.

As a small kid I had cats and dogs, of course; and the neighborhood was full of birds, chipmunks, and squirrels. But here, in the Barnum box, were huge wild animals that, miraculously, one could hold in his hand, snap in half, decapitate. Delicious animals, with a special chalky sweetness, that you could haul around in a handy box.

I've since done some further research—bought another box at the Great American store. I spread the animals out on my desk and counted twenty-one cookies and eighteen animals. (I got duplicate kangaroos and three gorillas.) And I

noted with interest that not all the animals were wild: for whatever reason, there was a sheep in that box.

Nabisco's been making animal crackers since 1902, and still uses, I think, the original molds. The animals have a stylized, turn-of-the-century look. (The last century, that is.)

Who, I wonder, was the marketing genius who thought of that cotton cord handle? My hand's too big to use it now; easier just to close fingers around the box. But for a little kid of three or four, it was perfect—and turned box and contents into possessions. "My box. My animal crackers," the child could say, clutching the string. Potent stuff, that.

But, dear Lord, I saw something else in my research—a second kind of box for Barnum's Animals in the Great American. Nabisco's gone politically correct! On its one side, the alternative box has three self-possessed animals looking you straight in the eye, over a low, vine-covered fence. Gorilla and elephant are gripping the fence—could push it over if they chose. And the lion seems poised to leap it. On the box's other side is the portrait of an endangered specimen, with facts about its size, preferred food, and native land.

That's fine, laudable, but I'm a traditionalist. I bought the 1902 version. And to better admire the handsome caged animals on its sides, I've kept the box on my desk.

You're right. It's empty now.

❖ ❖ ❖

All of our Fly Creek farmers have stories about head-strong, quirky animals. About the sweet-faced cow who watches for a chance to back-kick your shin. Or the billy goat who lowers his head at anything human. Or the goose who shows why its name also denotes a particular rude act.

A few years ago I heard my strange animal story across the ocean in Wales, while visiting cousins. Ewan and Sue, both medical doctors, are in love with country life. A few years ago, in the farmlands of North Wales, they bought the brick shell of an ancient barn. The two have worked hard and made it a warm, slate-roofed home for themselves and their children.

The family is animal-crazy and lives with a Noah's ark of them. Animals roam the house and fill the barnyard, outbuildings, and paddocks—dogs, cats, rabbits; a burro, a sagging old horse; geese, goats, pigs. And, of course, chickens.

The chickens free-range out of a decrepit shed: a dozen hens led by a glowering rooster. The hens are great layers, and Clovis the rooster guards them and their nests with paranoid zeal. Black-eyed and sharp of beak, he patrols the front of the shed, daring anyone to approach. Only Ewan risked collecting eggs, and did so carrying a cricket bat. Most days Clovis flew at his face and had to be batted away—not once, but repeatedly.

Tired of this—and worried for his children—Ewan telephoned to the next county. Living there, a neighbor had said, was a man famed for success with bad animals. A naturally gifted tamer.

Two mornings later, a tiny Morris Minor rattled up the farm road. Out climbed a round-shouldered, bow-legged little man in a patched worsted suit. He paused to put on a black bowler, and then crossed to Ewan, who is about six-foot-four. Eyes straight ahead, the man addressed Ewan's third shirt button.

"I will need," he intoned solemnly, "a large tub of water. That, and your rooster."

The kids ran to fetch the tub and fill it. Ewan went to the chicken shed, armed with the bat and a chicken-snatcher—a metal crook for snagging a chicken's leg. After a battle, he managed to snatch Clovis' legs from under him. Ewan carried him to the tamer upside down, squawking fiercely.

The solemn little man grasped Clovis' legs with both hands and suddenly plunged him into the tub, under water. One, two, three times, he slowly turned the struggling bird in clockwise circles, then raised him above the surface. Sputtering, outraged, Clovis squawked mightily and flapped his wings, throwing water everywhere.

The grim man didn't flinch. He plunged the bird back in. One, two, three times, he circled Clovis slowly by the legs, this time counterclockwise. Then, in one move, he yanked the bird out and hurled him free. Clovis described a long, shrieking arc and landed hard, twenty feet away, in a gorse bush. The tamer turned to Ewan's shirtfront.

"You'll have no more trouble with that bird," he said firmly. "Twenty pounds for professional service."

Whoa! That equates to over thirty dollars. But Ewan, much impressed, pulled out his wallet and paid him. The man nodded curtly and started for his car.

He didn't make it. With warlike scream, Clovis launched himself from the gorse bush and landed, sharp claws first, on the man's back. Bowler hat went flying as rooster beat him about the ears with heavy wings, pecked savagely the top of his balding head. Then, with a crow of triumph, the bird was gone again.

The little man stood stock still for a moment, cotton poking out of his suit's torn shoulder pads, blood welling from a dozen cuts. Then, without a word, he retrieved his hat, climbed in his car, was gone.

And Clovis? From that day, he was worse than ever. But, no matter, said Ewan. The show alone was worth the twenty pounds.

41

A Door Reopened,
a Lamp Relit

*G*reat news! In the heart of Fly Creek, we have a new old store. We had been without a hamlet grocery ever since Aufmuth's closed its doors over a year ago. Now the old place is open again, shelves stocked, and under a new name: Fly Creek General Store.

In Aufmuth's, we lost a grocery that had spanned three generations. And, like any country store, Aufmuth's had been much more than a place to buy goods and newspapers. Right at the hamlet's Four Corners, it was Fly Creek's social hub, where neighbors who shopped almost always tarried for news and gossip. Whether Aufmuth's heavy door was propped open in summer heat or closed tight against blustering cold, it was always an entry into the hamlet's life.

For nearly all the years I knew it, Aufmuth's was staffed by a pair of perfect foils. Jack Aufmuth, the owner, was a steadfast, laconic man; pleasant enough, but not one to waste a word. A joke to Jack would bring, at most, a tight smile and a raised eyebrow. Single-minded in devotion to the store, he presided over it from behind the meat counter, priding himself on roasts and chops cut to order.

For thirty years, Jack's clear opposite stood smiling at the register. Adolf Bider, known to most only as Duffy, was more than cashier. He was a genial entertainer, trading jokes and stories with the regulars. Duffy welcomed you to Aufmuth's like a host; his warmth made it an inviting place. And when finally his health broke and he had to retire, the store was like a lamp blown out. A few years after Duffy left, Jack died.

And not long after that, the store died, too. The door was locked, the windows dark.

Fly Creekers mourned the store when it closed, and most of us feared the worst. The site would be bought, we thought, by franchisers, who'd rip down the old clapboard building and clear the lot. Then they'd rivet together a steel frame, tack on aluminum skin, face the front with plastic and plate glass, light it up with neon. They'd give us back a store of sorts—and change Fly Creek forever.

That didn't happen. Tom Bouton bought the store, and he began to remake it—into what it had always been.

Tom's father owned several convenience stores in Oneonta, and Tom grew up in the business. He knows how to run a store—and he also loves old places. (His home's a converted carriage house in Gilbertsville.) So Tom set out to restore Aufmuth's—to its old self, and to us.

The worn oak floor's been stained dark, and sealed with the sheen it had when Duffy had just oiled it. From upstairs (the store's main selling floor earlier in the century), Tom has brought down an old oak counter—faced with tongue-and-groove and tipped in at the base, with a flat top worn smooth by hands and goods. Tom will stand behind it to greet you.

There are plenty of shelves and coolers, filled with the basics of any country grocery. And a counter for sandwiches, doughnuts, and coffee. And soon there'll be small tables where neighbors can sit and visit. It's a homey, welcoming place again.

When the front door again swung open for business, I can easily imagine that two distinct spirits glided in ahead of the first customers. One was Jack, straight-faced but nodding approval. The other was Duffy, beaming at his old home made new.

A lamp's been relit.

42

Eliphalet's House—and Ours

The find was as exciting for me, and as moving, as it was for the guests. They showed up in the late afternoon and, before they left, they had opened up new knowledge of our house.

I'd just brought Owen the cat back from Dr. Fassett's and a rabies booster. Owen had endured it like a stoic but was relieved to be back in Fly Creek. He hopped out as soon as I opened the truck door, and I followed, curious about a car parked on the house's far side.

Mike Hart, who's doing some carpentry for us, was talking with two well-dressed women. The pair turned out to be mother and daughter, the first from Connecticut and the second from New Jersey.

"Jim, maybe you can help these ladies," said Mike. "They're looking for an old house somewhere around here."

The women said they were questing a family home—from seven generations back. An ancestor had lived in Fly Creek back then, but all they had was a sepia photo of an old house, taken early in this century. They had the photo in hand; on its back, they said, were family names, including the very distant forebear's. When I asked the name, the mother pointed it out: Eliphalet Williams.

I grinned and hooked a thumb over my shoulder. "You've found his house."

Well, to Mike's delight and mine, those two dignified, well-dressed women let out whoops of excitement. We walked down the drive and stood right about where the old photo was taken. In the photo's foreground, leaning against a board fence long gone, was a serious young man in a stiff collar. Behind him loomed our house, sheathed in dark, weathered clapboard, its original two chimneys still in place. And off to his side, a range of hills looked exactly the same as when we raised eyes from the photo and glanced east, down the length of Allison Road.

Because of scholarly research by our Fly Creek neighbor Irene Dusenbery, I'd known Eliphalet's name at once. A very early owner of the stone mill that stood on Oaks Creek below our house, he ran it with great success until his death, at age forty-five, in 1817. (His family kept ownership till almost 1840.) Eliphalet's obituary said he left "a disconsolate widow bereft of a kind husband...the vicinity of a beneficent neighbor...the poor of a friend in need...the community of a useful

member and an honest man." That's someone I'd like to have known.

I toured the miller's kin through their ancestor's home, sharing in their excitement as they stood on wide floorboards that had once borne his weight, ran hands along the door frames he had leaned against, climbed narrow attic stairs he'd known well. And then I topped off their day.

"If you'll get in your car," I said, "I'll lead you up to Eliphalet's grave." We drove north, up Fly Creek Valley, to the Old

Chapel Burial Ground. Eliphalet's tall stone stands toward the back of the cemetery, with his daughter's alongside. The older woman rested a hand gently on it. We parted at the graveyard, and I drove back thinking of that good man, long dead, and of his house, now Anne's and mine.

In his life, Eliphalet had been as real to himself as I am to me—and he'd felt as much owner of the house and acreage as we now do. But we humans only pretend to own places and things. They are really just lent to us. Eliphalet sheltered awhile in the sturdy little house, and now we do. Others will come later and do the same.

And I thought, too, of an 1809 ad Irene had found in her research, placed by Eliphalet Williams in the Otsego Herald: An accidental fire, "communicated by a candle," had destroyed all his mill records for the season. And so Eliphalet petitioned "all those indebted to him for the aforementioned business, to come forward and make known the amount they are indebted, as soon as possible…" That's a poignant request, from an honest man in a bad fix.

It's late to worry about it, but I hope those debtors didn't bilk Eliphalet. I hope their better natures prevailed.

43

Raise the (Mailbox) Flag!

I opened the official United States Postal Service envelope and sighed. Otsego County's new 911 emergency system requires that every household have a street address. And so our Rural Delivery designation was now history, swept off to the ethereal dump of old numbers no longer used. No more RR 1, Box 9A. Our home's become 134 Allison Road. Too bad, but the 911 service will be worth it.

Getting the new address prodded me to take on a job that's been waiting since winter. Our mailbox post, rusted and decrepit after thirty years, had succumbed to the snowplows. Since the ground was too frozen in midwinter to put in a new post, I'd braced and wired the old one together to give shaky support to the box till spring.

Through the winter, I'd watched guiltily through the upstairs window by my desk as mailman Jim Ainslie pulled up out front. He'd wrestle with the wobbly box's rusty door—the whole thing nodding crazily at him as he collected our mailings and put our incoming in. Jim would frown at the box, and sometimes his lips would move. Couldn't tell what he said, of course.

And the wobbling wasn't Jim's only challenge. That box had been put up, thirty years before, by old Stan Stucin, who'd owned the place since World War II. Stan didn't stand very tall, and he positioned the box accordingly. Hence a long line of postmen, Jim the latest, have had to lean out over van windowsills, stretch 'way down to shove mail in. Over the years, I bet that's chafed a lot of armpits.

177

Feeling repentant, I vowed to do the new job right. I bought a big new box made of recycled plastic, with a matching plastic post designed to slide onto a pointed metal stake. "Easy to install!" its container blared in huge black type; and late one afternoon I rashly promised Anne she'd take the next day's mail out of the new box. To show my commitment, I started the job by tearing out the old box.

By dark, I still hadn't got the metal stake in the ground. Or, rather, I'd had it in the ground and out five times. Each time I'd hit a fresh rock that would slant or twist the stake, so the box would have ended up aimed skyward or turned broadside to the road. And all that pounding on the stake with a maul had dramatically reshaped its top. If metal stakes had mothers, this one's wouldn't have recognized it.

Feeling despondent, defeated, I worked on. Around nightfall Anne came out and led me in to something medicinal she'd made, over ice, with a slice of lime. That helped.

I was back out there after breakfast with pickax and shovel. I dug down three feet, set the stake with a level, tamped in rock and stones. Stage one done! Then I slipped the plastic post over the stake and tried to fasten the two together with carriage bolts.

The holes didn't match. My lips moved like Jim Ainslie's.

Later, I'd just been peering down the hollow post with a flashlight when my near neighbor Bill Shepard ambled down Cemetery Road.

"Hit a snag?" he asked with studied innocence. I told him the job had been all snags—that I'd actually started it the day before. Smiling slyly, Bill pointed at the flashlight. "At it all night, were you?"

The two of us then squatted by the post and discussed the problem in comforting guy talk—we talked torque, flanges, sleeves, lock washers, and such. We shifted the post on the stake this way, then that. We even read the instructions. And finally Bill passed judgment.

"They've missed drilling one hole in the stake. No fault of yours."

Oh, musical phrase! Bill went home for a metal-cutting bit, I to the barn for the drill. I'd—we'd—get this job done yet. And I'd be spared the humiliation that afternoon of making good my promise to Anne: There I'd stand, by the road, waiting for Jim Ainslie, with the new mailbox under my arm. Making a post of myself.

Later, I watched from my desk as Jim drove up to the new, rock-solid box. He smiled broadly as he reached—straight out—to put mail in it. His lips moved. I think I actually read the two words:

"About time!"

44

"Long Ago... Far, Far Away"

On my own across the weekend, I drove alone down to Oneonta to see the original, now-reissued *Star Wars*. I came home disappointed—in the movie, but more in me. The film's still good fun, but I guess twenty years of steadily better special effects have jaded all of us. This time, nothing took my breath away.

But maybe that's just twenty years of age on me. In days past, a powerful speech could pull me to my feet, get me stomping and whistling. A concert brass band or a mighty chorus could raise every hair on my neck, even bring tears. Not so any more; I just don't respond the way I once did. Why, in some areas of my life—well, any man my age could tell you. But won't.

Anyway, I liked *Star Wars,* even though Luke's rocketing into the Death Star didn't stop my breath as in the old days. And I did enjoy Harrison Ford—looking like a kid!—doing acting that was all grimace and swagger.

But the best entertainment for me was before the show, when the lights were still up. The theater was full of family groups, mostly thirtyish parents with young kids. Twenty years ago, the parents were their kids' age; now they were back to see *Star Wars* on the big screen again. And some of them, with real excitement, were telling their youngsters what a great show they'd see.

Two rows ahead of me a young pair was bracketing three little girls—five, four, and three, I'd guess. Mom, on the far inside, was talking quietly with Five. Dad, on the aisle, was entertaining Three and Four. Four, sitting dead center, had her boots off her feet and on her hands and forearms; she was facing me, trying to make the boots do a dance on the seat back. She wanted them to dance side by side; but elbows don't work that way, so she just made them kick one another's toes. Finally her dad gently pulled her around and down, by her little sister's side.

"Let me tell you about this movie," he said. "I saw it when I was a real little boy. I was not much older than you." Four rolled her eyes.

"Daddy, you weren't never little. You were always old!"

"Oh, yes, I was little," said Dad, easing the boots off her hands and putting them on the floor. "Once I was just Grandpa and Nana's tiny baby."

"A tiny baby?" repeated Four.

"Yep, a tiny baby."

"Did you wear diapers?" she asked.

"I sure did." Four squealed.

"Daddy had diapers!" she screamed, and that set off Three.

"Diapers!" Three shrieked. "Daddy! Diapers!" And, by way of embellishment, "Poo-Poo!"

Five was mortified. "Mommy, stop her!" she hissed. Mommy leaned across Five and Four, dragged Three over into her lap, whispering "Shhh! Shhh!" Daddy, red-faced, drew Four into his own lap. She was bent double, gasping with giggles.

"Now, you know that everybody starts off as a tiny baby," he said quietly. "Once you were our tiny baby, and before that, I was Nana's tiny baby—and, before that, Nana was her mother's tiny baby, too."

That big thought sobered Four. Giggles stopped. She stared at her father with round, thoughtful eyes.

"And someday," he said, "when you're grown, maybe you'll be mommy to a tiny baby girl, too. And maybe she'll grow up to have a baby, too." He paused. "And that tiny little baby will call you Nana!"

It was too much for Four. She threw herself against her father's chest, arms tight around his neck. Her eyes stared beyond me, not at the back of the theater, but at a new, huge spread of time. The past was not just yesterday, or last Christmas. The future—much more than tomorrow or next birthday. I watched as, thumb in mouth, she worked to understand, to find her place in all that time.

Three was still giggling in her mother's lap as the lights went down; but Four stayed quiet, pressed against her father's shoulder till he turned her and sat her on his lap, arms clasped around her. Then, in a gentle whisper, he read to his girls from the screen:

"Long ago, in a galaxy far, far away..."

45

"Where'd You Say You Live?"

But why Fly Creek? Folks living here are often asked that. And we take the question seriously. The official company line is that the name's origin is in the Dutch word vlie. That means "marsh or swamp;" and, after all, the creek which gives our hamlet its name does rise in a marsh about eight miles to the north. We shy away from the other logical explanation. There aren't a lot of flies on the creek or us. And besides, flies haul around a load of ugly associations: dirty, disease-ridden, parasitic, annoying. So we pretty much stick to the swamp story.

I'm minded of a story which, if it isn't true, certainly ought to be. The tale is about another place much farther west. Its name dated from that area's rough-and-tumble days. In fact, the name was replaced long ago by a more genteel one. The original was almost forgotten until the local, historically conscious theater group dredged it up as part of their own name: The Slit Gut Thespians.

But why Slit Gut? The locals out there had a company line, too: A very narrow channel of water is sometimes called a gut, and a particularly very narrow one might be called a slit gut. Their town, said the locals, had been named for such a stream. The fact that no stream passed through or near the town didn't faze them a bit. They had an answer to that one, too.

As the area had populated and more wells were dug, the skinny, little, narrow, tiny slit of a gut had dried up. Only the name remained, they said, a nostalgic reminder of their town's distant past. And so the local theater troupe painted it on a large sign and hung it over their refreshment stand.

That lobby sign was lettered in bright red in an antique type style. It read, "SLIT GUT THESPIANS." The long-gone gut was represented by a bilious-green line that branched and wound among the words. Twisting between "Slit" and "Gut," the snaky line looked to refreshment customers uncomfortably like a medical illustration. Profits at the counter were never very strong.

Actually, Slit Gut's name had an interesting real origin; too bad those folks didn't face up and flaunt it. The name was older than the town. It was first attached to a combination stage stop and saloon there, the only wooden building in fifty miles.

Back then, formal law hadn't arrived yet—though, as you'll see, a strong sense of fairness burned in some of the drunks and card players who spent their days in the bar. The place was named "McHawney's," after its owner. But not for long.

One day in 1852, a violent dispute developed at one of Mr. McHawney's card tables. A traveling gambler had been winning far too much from three frontiersmen. He had just cleverly relieved one of them of his last asset, a diamond ring. When the man, grieved and outraged, called the gambler a crook and demanded the jeweled ring back, the card shark had smiled slyly, popped the ring into his open mouth, and then swallowed it.

That, as it turned out, was a bad move. The other three dumped the table, grabbed the gambler, and hustled him out the door. Over his strong protests, they bent him backward over the hitching rail. There followed a piece of makeshift surgery that the gambler would have remembered the rest of his days, if he'd had some. The ring, of course, was recovered.

After that event, as you'd expect, the name "McHawney's" fell out of use. Stage drivers just told their passengers, "We'll stop at Slit Gut."

I wish we had such a story behind "Fly Creek." All we've got is the Dutch-settler explanation. And if we don't use that, we get identified with an ugly bug.

But wait. Maybe Fly, prefixing Creek, doesn't have to carry unpleasant associations. Maybe it can evoke lazy days spent by a shaded stream, watching the graceful play of insects over the surface. How about bright sunlight glinting on iridescent wings, slow circles flown over cool, smooth-running waters, with happy trout leaping to meet their little dinner companions?

As any number of marketers would say: Don't worry about the product. Dress up the package.

◆ ◆ ◆

Just now I have an interesting temporary job. Until the Fly Creek Valley Cemetery Association picks a new secretary, I've been pulled off regular Board membership and made secretary pro tem. That means, for the present, I'm temporary keeper of our post-office box, which I regularly check. And of the cemetery's winter vault, which I hope never to open. And temporary keeper of the Association's official seal, which dates from 1875. It's a heavy, somber device of black cast iron—looks like a control lever from Captain Nemo's "Nautilus."

The job also makes me custodian of the Cemetery records: dusty old ledgers (and, these days, also a computer printout), full of information. What's the Cemetery's population, you ask? Three thousand three hundred. That's sobering: It means we who (literally) live in Fly Creek are outnumbered by the departed ten times over. But not surprising, I guess: the Cemetery's been gathering tenants for a long time.

To scan those records is to see seventeen decades of Fly Creek's history, but not in buildings once built and then torn down, fields cleared and now grown over, businesses begun and later gone bust. It's to see the hamlet's seamless history

through interlocked lives. What I mean is this:

The first 'Creekers laid to rest there had known each other, and they had known the next generation, too. Then the next generation grayed and followed them—having known their elders, one another, and also those who followed them. So it was with the next generation. And so it's continued right to the present.

Human links are what makes a country cemetery different from one in a city, where strangers lie in adjoining graves, just as strangers live in adjoining city apartments. No strangers lie side by side in Fly Creek Valley Cemetery. It is no less a community than the living hamlet is. And, in fact, the two are truly melded.

For we humans are as much nurture as nature, molded as much by one another as by genetics. The human contacts we've had, for good or ill, have shaped what we are today. And not just close contacts, with family or friends. The smiling grocer who once patted you on the head at four, in a minute but real way, shaped you: he made the world seem kinder, safer. The second-grade teacher who snapped impatiently at you shaped you, too: she made it seem the opposite. In values and attitudes, we're all products of such contacts, beyond counting.

That means that today's long-time Fly Creekers, who knew many, many now in the Cemetery, are living lives formed by them—through countless thousands of past contacts. And through those they knew, they're linked to still earlier 'Creekers, who were shapers (and were shaped) in their own time. Thus Cemetery and hamlet form a community whose humans bonds tie all together, across all the years—those still traveling the roads, and those gathered under the trees in wordless, timeless communion.

I'm not long in Fly Creek but I already have friends buried in that Cemetery—dear friends who surely influenced and formed me. And through those few, I'm tied now into that vast, quiet assemblage, right back to its beginnings.

I like that thought. And I'm glad that, just now, I help watch out for them.

46

Not an Earthquake—
Just a Cultural Shift

If you felt a ground tremor around here the first weekend of May, don't worry. It was just the county's cultural hub shifting to Fly Creek.

Oh, I know that Cooperstown's got a claim on being Otsego County's arts center, what with the Glimmerglass Opera and the concert series and such. And Oneonta, with two colleges and their cultural lives, could argue for it, too. But the hamlet of Fly Creek beats them, flat out. We've got the Philharmonic.

Do I sense raised eyebrows? Well, wait a minute. With a Fly Creek Philharmonic performance, we're not talking about enduring a couple of hours of painful amateurism. Theirs isn't the kind of program you bear with for the sake of a good cause, or because your kids are going to tap dance, or because you brother, the undiscovered stand-up comic, is going to do his shtick. I'm talking about entertainment, largely musical, of amazing quality; and every bit of it produced in Fly Creek, by Fly Creekers.

The hamlet is home, you see, to a dozen fine singers and instrumentalists, people of real professional skill. And they've drawn into their company an added two dozen talented locals. Under Susan Rodd's artistic direction, this group regularly entertains sold-out houses in the Fly Creek Methodist Church. Their programs may include classical guitar, music hall patter songs, instrumental trios, funky ragtime by the Fuzzy Logic Jug Band, and often a truly fine kazoo choir.

Yes, kazoos. One Philharmonic program opened with a fanfare from the church loft: a dozen kazooists playing Mouret's

"Rondeau" (that's the "Masterpiece Theater" theme). They played, not in unison, but from an orchestral score: kazoos, mind you, in rich, intricate harmony. Pitch was clear, tempo crisp, dynamics subtly defined. Kazoos! They sounded like— what?—a whole hive of blessedly gifted bees. At the end of the "Rondeau," people clapped, they laughed, they wiped away tears of delight.

But what happened on that recent May weekend—what gave a final shove to the cultural shift—was the Fly Creek Philharmonic's latest concert, which premiered Sam Wilcox's "Pavane for a Dead Cow." (Yes, Sam does live in Cooperstown— but you notice he chose Fly Creek for the premiere.)

Even before that concert, the Fly Creek Philharmonic, featured two years before on Garrison Keillor's "Prairie Home Companion," had gained a national audience. I should say international, since Canadian and English friends tell us "PHC" broadcasts are much loved across the border and even across the ocean. Indeed, who knows? Perhaps, two years ago, the Queen herself may have enjoyed the Philharmonic, seated by the royal radio, primly smiling in bathrobe, slippers, and crown.

The past weekend's concert had all the Philharmonic's signature elements—some serious music performed with real artistry, great participation by spirited kids, creative instrumentation (flutes, kazoos, string bass, piano, tin whistle, triangle, tambourines, xylophones, castanets). Plus wit, whimsy, even slapstick.

The evening's openers, Sam Wilcox's three pieces for classical guitar, were played perfectly by Catherine Mason and Richard Salsa. I liked all three—but the first one included an ethereal dialog between guitars that left me breathless with its beauty.

Later came the kids' mini-drama cum music, bracketed by adults singing "Mister Sandman," "Three Little Maids From School," and "Heart and Soul." And followed later by a parody

seventeenth-century madrigal titled, "My Bonnie Lass She Smelleth." The madrigal was sung in complex five-part harmony, with enough cascading fa-la-la's to last till the cows come home.

Speaking of which:

The program's second half was Sam's epic "Pavane for a Dead Cow," performed by full eclectic orchestra, by soloists, by large costumed chorus. And by the audience who, though unrehearsed, moo'd soulfully on cue and to great effect.

Principal parts went to Bill Hayes as grieved Farmer Joe and to Karen Schlather as a soprano who kept elbowing out from an annoyed chorus to wring more pathos out of every motif. Dolly Belle, the star-crossed, lightning-struck cow, neither spoke nor sang. She was represented by a painting of a large Jersey whose molten dark eyes seemed lit with foreknowledge of her own cruel fate.

I was, you might guess, very taken by the "Pavane." Except for one part near the climax that made me uneasy. The chorus was consoling poor Farmer Bob by singing that Dolly Bell, though gone, awaited him in the afterlife. And then they all raised eyes and pointed upward—not over their own heads, but out over the audience.

More than once over the years, reckless birds have bespattered me. So I'm really edgy about cows overhead.

That moment aside, the evening was superb. What a shame, though, that the concert wasn't broadcast—so Her Britannic Majesty could have shared the fun.

Sorry, your Majesty, but for this one Buckingham Palace wouldn't do. You had to be in Fly Creek.

47

Keeping Watch
with the Flock by Night

I did it last Christmas Eve. I will repeat it tonight. Maybe it has become my personal Christmas ritual. Sheep are involved, and an old kerosene lantern.

You already know the sheep. Maggie, Mary, Olive, and Pearl are comfortably settled into the south-facing shed, free to wander out into their paddock and then back to a full hay rack and a heated water tub. They're entertaining company just now—a rent-a-ram named Alf, here for the month through the kindness of the McCormacks of Christian Hill.

I first worried a bit about Alf—he didn't swing into action, and spent a lot of time just standing around with a dreamy, distant look in his eyes. Alf reminded me of my undergraduate philosophy prof. While walking the campus, that man would sometimes slow, then stop dead, his eyes glazed, his mind lost in deep abstractions. But then I remembered something. Despite his unworldly air, the professor had six sturdy, healthy kids. So I've stopped worrying about Alf.

The lantern I mentioned is an old, railroad-style one. It hung in my grandparents' Annapolis cellar, then my parents', now ours. Through my boyhood, it was brought out for power failures and other emergencies—it did yeoman service the September that Hurricane Hazel rolled relentlessly up the Chesapeake. Hazel ripped up docks, threw boats ashore, tore off house roofs and shutters; she left us powerless for almost a week. I remember those black, humid nights and that old lantern's comforting glow.

Since moving north, I've broken it out for a few blackouts

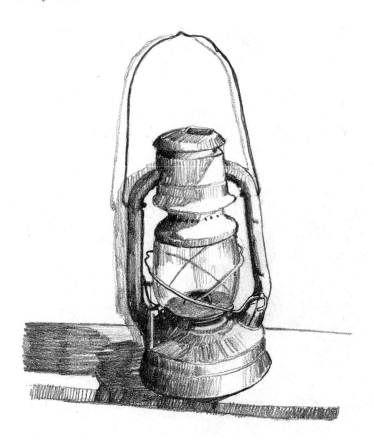

here; and last winter year, I lit it again. It was Christmas Eve and ten o'clock—time for the sheep's bed-check. My flashlight batteries were dead. I could have looked for another flashlight; getting out the lantern was a whim.

But maybe not. Raising the pitted glass shade and touching match to wick, I thought of loving hands, long gone, that had done the same. (Christmas often brings such thoughts, doesn't it?) I blessed their memory and closed the shade.

Walking out to the sheep shed, I moved in an orb of golden light that spread and thinned across the snow. At the small shed, I opened the door and stepped inside. The ewes had settled down along the walls in the straw. They looked up, curious, as I hung the lantern from a low rafter.

Furniture out in the shed is pretty sparse: just the manger, the hayrack, the water tub—and for me, a folding chair for use at lambing time. Perhaps on another whim, I opened the chair and, still under the sheep's bland gaze, settled into it.

The lantern's honeyed light fell gently on old walls, straw-covered floor, the animals' wool. In each of the black window-panes, the orange flame was mirrored like a distant, pinpoint star. It was blessedly quiet—just a faint wind around the eaves and an occasional low throat-clearing by one of the ewes.

I had sat there perhaps fifteen minutes when Maggie, the matriarch, rose—onto her elbows, then back end up, then shoulders and head. As if on signal, the other three arose, too, and followed Maggie to form a semicircle in front of me. They stood mute, gazing, wordlessly communing. Then Maggie, who loves to be scratched, stepped forward and put her broad head on my knee. I dug my curled fingers deep into the wool and scratched between her ears.

It was a fine moment, I thought—a wondrous one. It came to me that this small shed, with manger and straw; this soft golden light; these dense, earthy smells; this blessed quiet; these gentle beasts—it was the very setting of the Nativity story. For a moment of held breath, I could almost expect a sound from outside—low voices, a donkey's slow clop. But no. That was far away, not here. And long, long ago.

Still, I've found a very good place to be on Christmas Eve.

48

Two Great Parades

A pair of kids, twenty years ago. They come to mind every time I watch a Memorial Day Parade. I recall them with great affection and always will.

At noon on a very hot holiday, my late first wife Gwen and I were visiting in a hamlet around here. We'd gone with our hosts to watch the local parade and stood waiting on a shady porch just next to the central school. The parade was on its way; from three blocks down the street; we could hear the school band coming. They were playing, more or less, Sousa's "Washington Post March."

This was the day's finale for the tired bandsmen, who'd already been bussed to two other bandless communities for parades—one at nine, a second at half-past ten. They'd wolfed down bag lunches on the bus trip back, and now they were marching down the home stretch, toward their own school and one final invocation and "Star Spangled Banner," one last stem-winder speech and "Taps."

Here came the parade, and predictably, it was a delight: marching boy and girl scouts, hopping, every so often, to get in step; spiffy firemen with pikes and antique axes; gold-star mothers driven in an open Caddy; the year's Dairy Queen in her prom dress, shyly waving and blushing prettily; youngsters astride ponies with plaited manes.

At the end came boys on bicycles with bits of cardboard clothes-pinned into their spokes—to make a Harley rumble. Oh, and in the parade's middle, the band, twenty strong; sweating along in their pegged pants, tight red coats with

196

epaulettes and frogging up the front, and stiff-brimmed cylindrical caps.

"There's Lynne," said our friends' pre-teen, next to me at the porch rail. She pointed at a thin-faced clarinetist in the first row, with harlequin glasses and a too-big cap pushing down her ears. Lynne was blowing and fingering earnestly as she passed.

"You'd never know, would you?" added the pre-teen.

"What?" I asked.

"She doesn't have a reed."

Lynne, it seemed, hadn't been long at the clarinet; and when she practiced, the screeches she produced set dogs howling and cows bellowing on neighbors' farms. So, for the Memorial Day parades, they'd taken away her reed. She was allowed to march and mimic music-making. But, for all the fingerwork and blowing, Lynne's woodwind made only a thin, hardly audible whoosh.

I watched her as the band formed up in the hot sunshine in front of the school, and as she mimed her way through another "Star-Spangled Banner."

That's dedication, I thought. That's a spunky girl.

The day's high point, it turned out, belonged to another red-faced, sweating youngster. He was in the band's back row. Why, I wonder, does the chunky kid nearly always end up with the sousaphone? This broad-faced, freckled boy of fourteen looked typecast: His torso strained the band jacket's buttons, and his sousaphone's brass coils looked like they'd been soldered in place around him.

He caught my attention halfway through the patriotic speech—when the sousaphone's bell began to waver, flashing in the sun.

That kid's going to faint, I thought, evidently just as that idea rose woozily in his own head. He broke from the back row and staggered toward the shade—a slow-motion, tip-toe run, his weight well ahead of his shoes, and that looming

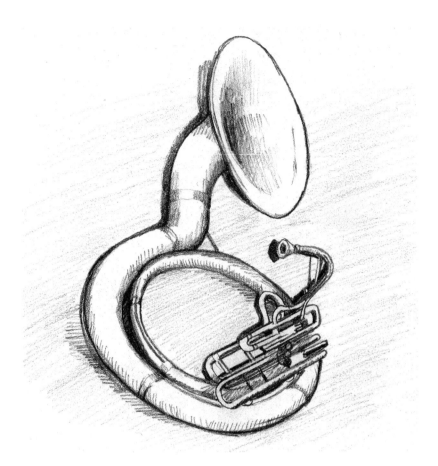

bell seeming to drag him on. Then, down he crashed on his face and rolled slowly over, sousaphone pointing skyward.

Four people ran from the crowd to help. The upstaged speaker lost his audience. The boy was out cold, and everyone watched the four struggle to divest him of that sousaphone. Perhaps it had bent in the crash, clutching him even more tightly. Two pulled on the bell and one on each foot, but nothing would give.

Maybe, I thought, they'll have to get the rescue squad—a job for the "jaws of life."

But just then the four gave a mighty, concerted yank and he came loose, limp arms sliding last through the brass coils.

Revived, he was led, hobbling, off the field. We all applauded in sympathy, of course—though when someone else carried off the sousaphone, we applauded him, too.

Brave Lynne the clarinetist and that nameless red-faced boy—in their mid-thirties now. I wonder, have they forgotten that hot Memorial Day?

Not me. Never will.

❖ ❖ ❖

It was a great idea, though we nearly drowned ourselves doing it.

Jim Fish proposed that the Fly Creek Area Historical Society have a float in the Springfield July Fourth Parade, and we all agreed at once. Jim would use his four-wheeler to tow a flatbed wagon. On it we'd put a table, chairs, and a half-dozen Society members. With the group dressed in country clothes and a gavel on the table, we hoped the tableau would suggest a meeting in progress.

Just a reminder to the community of one of its organizations. Nothing dramatic.

It got dramatic on Parade Day. At nine, just as Jim pulled the wagon onto Frank Smith Road and I arrived with a truck loaded with table and chairs, the rain came, too. We hauled everything to Jim's son's home in the village, planning to finish the float under cover in his garage. The rain eased, then ended.

By ten-thirty the float was ready—tri-color bunting tacked around the hay wagon, signs on staffs touting the Society and its goals, and even a colonial-style stars-and-stripes flown off the stern. Chairs, tables, and people in place, we chugged out of the driveway and headed toward the marshaling site, to take our place in the line.

There we waited, just in front of the Milford School contingent, really nice kids in purple and white: the school band, a uniformed color guard with pretend rifles, and about eighteen vaguely Delphic-looking maidens—flowing white gowns with purple sashes and headbands. As they waited, the maidens practiced graceful sweeps with spangled hoops and lavender flags. They were charming and, as I say, seemed to evoke classic Greece as much as Milford.

Florence Michaels and I had the best view of them: we were seated behind the table, facing our fake meeting. We could see down the whole line of march—and also see what was piling up the sky behind it.

On the flatbed, we talked and joked and pretended not to notice the sudden twilight. But soon we were beyond pretending. Big raindrops splattered down. With squeals and giggles, the Milford kids broke ranks and crowded under a maple next to our float. We oldsters just held our places and told one another it would soon stop.

It didn't. At eleven, parade and rain took off in earnest; by the time our float swung onto the main street, everything and everybody on board was soaked. And this was a cold rain, mind you, with some wind behind it.

I'm sure the parade planners had seen those clouds rolling in. But the year before, the parade had been drowned out—no parade in Springfield Center for the first time in fifty years. So I think those first splatters brought, not wavering, but a stiffening of wills: Be damned if we'll be rained out two years in a row! We're going to have a parade!

And that, wondrously, was the mood of everyone, including us soaked Fly Creekers. And including the crowd, who, by the hundreds, held their places. People sheltered under umbrellas of every size and color. (I caught just a glimpse of my Anne in her yellow sou'wester.) Whole families huddled under tarps and plastic sheets, grinning, waving back at us, laughing along with us.

For we laughed hard at ourselves the whole length of the parade—a wagonload of antique furniture and fairly antique people, pretending to hold a meeting as cold torrents poured over them. I think that I laughed myself to tears, though it would've been hard to tell.

Dot Martin's sodden poke bonnet slowly collapsed around her face like a morning glory closing for the night. Periodically, Pete Martin would tip his felt hat, and its rim would spill water like an eaves-trough. And behind us, out beyond our dripping, drooping flag, I could see the Milford kids, tootling along bravely. The hoops and lavender flags flung sheets of spray as the girls twirled them.

Afterward, we slogged back to Tim's on foot, laughing still. What we'd done had been absurd, but glorious. And, looking for Anne in the dispersing crowds, I thought I'd never seen happier faces.

I'd hate to have missed that miserable soaking. Freedom and community are great to celebrate, wet or dry.

49

Following the Sign

About thirty-five hundred miles east of Fly Creek, across the Atlantic, a weathered sign hangs on the back of a shed. The shed is in Wyche Marine, a complex of docks, open shops, and boats hauled up for repair. The boatyard spreads alongside a broad, sheltered harbor, down on England's south coast.

Twenty-four centuries ago, the harbor was sailed by ships of colonizing Romans. They had their major headquarters at the harbor's north end: mosaics from the governor's palace there are still being unearthed. Today's boats belong to weekend sailors who heel and tack on the harbor's broad waters and even venture out its mouth, into the English Channel. The boatyard does good business meeting sailors' needs, as does the pub next to it. That pub and the locale are both called Dell Quay.

The weathered sign is posted on the back end of a boatyard shed, the land side. Others like it are posted throughout the yard. This one speaks tersely to walkers skirting the back of the yard, heading up the shoreline path toward the Roman palace ruins.

A man I know first read that sign ten years ago. His wife had died, and the Maryland college where they'd both worked had mercifully sent him off on a sabbatical. He spent most of it in England. Part of his time there he hiked alone, trying to order his spirit.

His wife's cancer had been over a year killing her, perhaps because she had fought against it so bravely. Many times during the year, sometimes even as the man bathed her or changed dressings, an awful thing occurred. He'd catch himself thinking beyond her certain death—thinking of himself, of what was to become of him. And each time he'd feel hot shame. How could any part of him not be right there, sharing in her pain?

But despite his shame, questions kept coming. What would he do? How could he stay in the house they'd shared? How could he continue in his work, which now seemed hollow, drained of meaning?

Then came the end, and after it, the trip abroad and the hiking alone. That wounded man went odd, sometimes cried as he walked. He talked a lot half aloud, sometimes to his dead wife, mostly to himself. To himself, he kept saying the same thing: Poor fool, what are you going to do now?

There was, of course, their small retreat up in rural New York, a place he loved. The man had worked enough years to retire and move there. He'd have money enough, in his pension and his wife's, at least to begin a new life.

But was he brave enough? Could he cut ties? Could he leave a job, good pay, respect—leave hometown and friends? Did he dare launch out, alone?

One noonday the man's walking brought him to Dell Quay. In the quiet pub he had a ploughman's lunch and a pint of bitters, staring out at the pewter-colored water. Then he left the pub and started up the path along the east shore, behind the boatyard. And saw the weathered sign.

"A found poem," the man thought. (He knew a found poem is plain writing, even graffiti, that reads like poetry—because of rhyme, perhaps, or rhythm or imagery.) But then he read the wooden board again and sensed more. It was a message. To him. In three lines, nine words, the sign said,

> *Boats are stored*
> *berthed or moored*
> *at owner's risk.*

The literal meaning was clear enough—a legal disclaimer by Wyche Marine. But to this odd man, wandering, groping for answers, the sign said something else.

Danger lies, it said, in choosing safety—in storing one's boat ashore, or roping it to the dock, or chaining onto a buoy close to shore. True, the boat would be secure. But it would be useless. As long as it was safe, it would go nowhere.

Boats are stored
berthed or moored
at owner's risk.

The man pondered the message. And decided, no. He could

not choose security. Whatever the unknown, he'd have to cast off, get under way. And so, thank God, he did.

I want to stand by my Anne's side as she reads that weathered sign. For, like me, she knows that man well.

An Afterword

I moved to Fly Creek alone. Pancreatic cancer—savage, implacable—had taken Gwen, my wife of eighteen years.

We'd met as new faculty members at the same college, just outside Annapolis, Maryland. We'd married, endured the heartbreak of repeated miscarriages, decided finally that we were meant to do our parenting through our teaching.

We were very happy for seventeen years. Then came the cancer, a year and a half of suffering, and she was gone. I stayed in my deanship for a couple more years, numbed by loss. Then I decided that, without some move, I'd idle in neutral the rest of my days. So I took early retirement, sold the house we'd shared, and moved four hundred miles north to rural New York State.

Gwen had grown up there, and I'd fallen in love with its rolling hills as soon as I saw them. A dozen years into our marriage, we had bought an old house and ten acres in Fly Creek, twelve miles from her childhood home. We planned to retire there together, but now I was headed in that direction, thinking I would spend the rest of my life alone.

In retrospect, I was fleeing grief; but then I was only sure that my future lay up there. I did know that a house two centuries old needed renovation, and I had vague ideas about raising vegetables and some farm animals. I headed for the tiny hamlet of Fly Creek, thinking I'd live a hermit's life. I expected to end up as the odd, kindly old coot at the end of Cemetery Road.

But living there, both in the tiny community and among the mute animals, brought me back to a shared life. I learned from the animals' daily dependence on me, and from watching and sitting quietly among them. I learned from the people and the patterns of the hamlet. I entered a very happy marriage. I came back to life.

—Jim Atwell

A Maryland native, Jim Atwell spent thirteen years as a Catholic teaching monk. In 1969, he went back to Annapolis and took a faculty position at Anne Arundel Community College. In his twenty-three years there, he was successively professor, chairman, dean, and vice president.

Jim owes his deep love of New York's Leatherstocking Country to his late first wife Gwen, who grew up near Cooperstown. After Gwen's death, he moved north to start life again in an old farmhouse they had bought there. A few years later he remarried; Jim Atwell and Anne Geddes-Atwell still make their home in Fly Creek, raising sheep, pigs, and chickens.

Artist and graphic designer Anne Geddes-Atwell created the layout for this book and drew the illustrations. She was born in Calgary, Alberta, Canada, and holds masters degrees in fine arts and art history. She has run a pair of successful graphic design businesses: In Cahoots, Inc. in Annapolis and Stone Mill Graphic Design in Fly Creek.

More information about Jim's freelance writing is available at www.JimAtwell.com.